John

Saints by Our Side

John of the Cross

By George P. Evans

BOOKS & MEDIA
Boston

Library of Congress Cataloging-in-Publication Data

Names: Evans, George P. (George Peter), author.

Title: John of the Cross / by George P. Evans.

Description: Boston, MA : Pauline Books & Media, 2017. | Series: Saints by our side series | Includes bibliographical references.

Identifiers: LCCN 2017021335| ISBN 9780819840196 (pbk.) | ISBN 081984019X (pbk.)

Subjects: LCSH: John of the Cross, Saint, 1542-1591. | Christian saints--Spain--Biography.

Classification: LCC BX4700.J7 E93 2017 | DDC 271/.7302 [B] --dc23

LC record available at https://lccn.loc.gov/2017021335

In the book, *God Speaks in the Night,* all the quotes are mentioned as from ICS Publications.

Cover design by Rosana Usselmann

Cover art by Francisco de Zurbaran, 1656
Background: istockphoto.com/© KingWu

Published by Pauline Books & Media, 50 Saint Pauls Avenue, Boston, MA 02130-3491

Printed in the U.S.A.

www.pauline.org

Pauline Books & Media is the publishing house of the Daughters of St. Paul, an international congregation of women religious serving the Church with the communications media.

1 2 3 4 5 6 7 8 9 21 20 19 18 17

Contents

. . . .

Introduction

People feel more easily drawn toward some saints, for example Saint Francis, the poor, humble man of Assisi; or Saint Thérèse of Lisieux, the splendid Little Flower in God's garden. But they are less likely to feel drawn to someone who is named after the Cross. And even more so if that saint is someone described as "perhaps one of the most misquoted and misunderstood of all the writers in the Christian spiritual canon."[1]

Saint John of the Cross is such a saint. And while his name and writings might make him seem intimidating, he deserves to be better known. He was a Carmelite priest, a poet, a theologian, a trusted and prudent spiritual director, and a leader in his religious order. He became one of the world's foremost experts on the dynamics of making progress in faith, prayer, and love. Partly due to his very name, he tends to command respect for taking the Christian way of life seriously. However, other factors have led to him being misunderstood: his depth of teaching, his mysterious poems, and his forthright dealing with the darker, harder side of following Christ. As the Carmelite scholar Kieran Kavanaugh has noted regarding John's writings: "[his] is a treasure difficult to mine."[2] John of the Cross is underappreciated as a model of how ordinary folks can follow Christ. Some have prejudged him as a forbidding over-achiever in the sanctity department or have presumed that they cannot relate to his story.

Early written portrayals of John by supporters of his cause for canonization stressed his unusual holiness and emphasized the extraordinary features of his life. They depicted him as so rigorous in his penances, unreachable in his theological ideas, and proficient in prayer that the average Christian could not hope to imitate him. His biographers underplayed what John holds in common with most spiritual wayfarers.

After being declared a Doctor of the Church in 1926, a new and more accessible image of John slowly emerged. The former view of John has not completely faded, but a new perspective on his life and gifts has helped bring him further into the mainstream of Christian spirituality.

Today his life deserves a fresh look. Those willing to get to know John will find that his depth and seriousness are matched by his joy and honesty. His life story, versatile gifts, and proven insights lead one into the riches that come from following Christ wholeheartedly. With John, Christian life is never static but always moves toward a more profound relationship with God. John wants us to know, love, and serve the God whose friendship he deeply prized. John stands out among the saints as one who meets people where they are and speaks from his own experience of the beauty and messiness of life. We don't need to keep John on a pedestal; he can be, in the words of this series, one of the "saints by our side."

John let himself be surrounded by love, even when his life was difficult. The love he lived, taught, and offered was not fluffy or superficial, but the self-sacrificing, sometimes tough love he saw modeled and freely given by Jesus Christ, our Savior.

To celebrate the 400th anniversary of John's death, Saint John Paul II wrote *Master in the Faith*, a tribute to the witness John still offers the Church. In this document, the pope discusses the virtue of faith as understood by John of the Cross. Saint John Paul reminds us that John "speaks to the deepest aspirations of the human person" (no. 1) and calls John's writings "a treasure to be shared with all those who seek the face of God today" (no. 1).[3]

Saint John has been an ever more familiar companion of my life. In my childhood I remember John as one of the saints I read about in the book *Heavenly Friends: A Saint for Each Day*.[4] I was impressed with his story, but I didn't hold on to many details.

As a seminarian, I enrolled in a wonderful course that each week explored the teachings of an acclaimed Christian spiritual master. John and his friend Teresa of Ávila were included. I found the short introduction to John's life story intriguing but his teachings hard to understand. I wish I had known his life more fully before tackling his ideas.

A few years later, as I began studying for my doctorate in theology at The Catholic University of America, I participated in a fine seminar course that surveyed the major Christian spiritual masters. The course included three prominent Carmelite saints: Teresa, John, and Thérèse of Lisieux. That same year, the university hosted a three-day symposium commemorating the 500th anniversary of Saint Teresa of Ávila's death. This event introduced me to research from leading scholars. I never forgot my pleasant exposure to Teresa and her friend John, and I have always retained my esteem for them.

Later, as a spiritual director on the faculty of Saint John's Seminary in Boston, I relied on some of Saint John's helpful insights. While many of my colleagues were versed in the contribution of Ignatius of Loyola and the Jesuit tradition, I investigated other strains of our Catholic spiritual legacy. Remembering the two great sixteenth-century Carmelite superstars, and less daunted by John's teachings than before, I developed a course, which I have often taught. It considers the life and teachings of Teresa, John, and their spiritual daughter Thérèse. I am glad to help people discover how all three saints speak so convincingly of the gift of God's love for each of us and of our reciprocal self-gift to God.

While many classic spiritual writers present particular elements of the Christian's spiritual quest, John is outstanding in his comprehensive description of spiritual development. Moreover, John is unsurpassed in his ability to deal with the tougher side of trying to live as a Christian. He addresses issues such as our own resistance to grace as well as our unhelpful attachments and challenges, in maturing into better ways of prayer, letting go of blocks to growth, and dealing with suffering. John's mastery of these matters makes him an exceptionally realistic spiritual guide. He knew the power of the paschal mystery: the death and resurrection of Christ. Evident in John's life and teaching, this paschal pattern has helped me to understand my own journey with God and to accompany others on theirs. John has become a guide and one of my favorite "heavenly friends." And I am happy to introduce others to the life of this remarkable saint.

The saints lived in our world with their own hopes and worries, stories and struggles, temptations and talents, and they let God's love fill them. God's grace keeps flowing out through them to us. May John, God's friend and mine, become a friend to those who get to know him better. May meeting John through his personal story be a springboard to exploring his teachings.

Chapter One

A Tough Start in Life

Gonzalo de Yepes and Catalina Álvarez, the parents of the man now acclaimed as Saint John of the Cross, were a devoted but struggling Catholic couple in sixteenth-century Spain. Their roots were in the Toledo area, within the region of Castile. While virtually untouched by the upheaval of the Reformation that had rocked much of Europe, Spain had earlier experienced its own religious and cultural divisions. In the early eighth century, Arab Muslims conquered much of predominantly Christian Spain. After that, Christians, Muslims, and Jews lived together rather peacefully, albeit separately. A few centuries later, benefitting from disunity among the Muslims, separate Christian kingdoms emerged in northern and central Spain. They expanded southward and reasserted Catholicism. The last Muslim holdout was the region of Granada in Spain's far south, but in 1492 the staunchly Catholic Spanish monarchs Ferdinand and Isabella conquered that area.

A century earlier, in 1391, a tragic persecution of Jews had erupted, and this caused many Jews to become Christians by force. Known as *conversos,* they often became successfully integrated into Spanish society. However, "old Catholics" harbored suspicion toward them. Under Ferdinand and Isabella, the many thousands of remaining Jews in Spain were ordered to convert to Catholicism by 1492 or face expulsion. Nationalistic fervor prevailed. Many practicing Jews chose to leave Spain, but many others stayed and converted. Likewise, the monarchs brought about the mass conversion of Muslims, who were called *moriscos.* Into and throughout the sixteenth century a widespread but largely unfounded suspicion grew that many of the converted Jews and Muslims were secretly maintaining their former religious practices. Many people focused on the prestige of having pure Spanish blood, which led them to disparage the *conversos* and *moriscos.*

Gonzalo de Yepes was a young man descended from a prominent line of silk merchants, but he had been an orphan. He worked as an administrative clerk and a cloth salesman in a business owned by his uncles. During his travels, Gonzalo met and fell in love with Catalina Álvarez, a poor weaver and also an orphan. She was boarding at a weaving shop in Fontiveros, a small town in Castile between Ávila and Salamanca. Their desire to marry sprang from a genuine love and not from any hopes of gaining property or wealth. Love emboldened Gonzalo to give up a potentially secure future in exchange for the unknown. In 1529, despite their different backgrounds, the two freely gave themselves to each other in marriage. Sadly, however, Gonzalo's previously supportive relatives immediately disowned him. Social standing and ethnic background meant a lot in sixteenth-century Spain.

The rejection by his relatives, a situation Gonzalo bravely suffered, may have stemmed from economic differences, but another line of interpretation ascribes it to his being of mixed Spanish-Jewish descent. His marriage to Catalina, a woman possibly of Arab-Muslim background, and definitely from a lower economic class, could only further harm his family's reputation. Whatever the truth of their backgrounds, these newlyweds faced a hard life.[1] With a resilience born of love, Gonzalo moved into his wife's boarding house and did what he could to help her at the loom and to sell their wares.

Later, Catalina and Gonzalo settled into a modest house in Fontiveros. Over the course of a dozen years, they welcomed three sons. Francisco was born in 1530, and John (Juan) in 1542.[2] At some time between those years, the middle son, Luis, was born. The family struggled economically, but they had a happy home, "where love had priority over material goods and sharing over accumulation."[3]

The family's situation changed for the worse when a serious illness struck Gonzalo. Catalina devoted herself to assisting her husband during his long decline. He died when John was just a toddler. A crisis arose after his death. Bereft of Gonzalo's love and financial support, Catalina and her boys struggled to survive. Families like John's, headed by a single mother who tried to eke out an existence as a weaver, were easily overlooked and left to founder.

As a child, John lived with his family on the fringes of society during Spain's "Golden Age," a term masking the severe poverty that also existed. Spain had become a political, religious, and cultural force in the world. It had sent explorers to the New World. Commerce and agriculture thrived, but with a limited distribution of wealth. Despite its riches and power, Spain spent much of its resources to fund its conflicts with foreign forces. The treasures pouring in from the New World reached the prosperous, more established populace, but not the impoverished masses who suffered from discrimination, unhealthy conditions, and unemployment. During the 1540s, central Spain entered "the barren years," a time of poor harvests in Castile, which resulted in a downward spiral of resources for the needy.

For a time the young widow Catalina served as a paid wet nurse for her infant niece. But with the hope that Gonzalo's brothers in Toledo would help their nephews, she set out on the difficult 110-mile journey with her three sons. Desperate for adequate food and security, they probably had to beg along the way. Despite the beautiful countryside of fields, hills, and valleys, Catalina must have worried about their survival.

One of the boys' uncles, a clergyman (archdeacon) in Toledo, quickly dashed Catalina's hopes by sending her away. We can only wonder what effect the hard-heartedness of this man of God had on John. Maybe his memory of that rejection readied him to experience the need to love the Church realistically despite its imperfect and sinful members.

Sad but undaunted, Catalina and her sons made their way to nearby Galvez to see Gonzalo's other brother, Juan de Yepes, a married medical doctor who then had no children. This visit stirred their hopes. Juan de Yepes offered to house, educate, and leave his fortune to Francisco. Francisco was far from intellectually talented, but this generous overture seemed to guarantee him a promising future. A relieved Catalina and her younger sons bid a sad farewell to Francisco and then made the long journey home to Fontiveros.

As often happens in situations rooted in desperation, Francisco soon grew to dislike his new home. He suffered under the almost slave-like conditions to which his uncle's wife subjected him. She surreptitiously blocked his education. When Catalina did not hear from Francisco, she painstakingly returned to Toledo to check on him. What she found made her determined to bring him home to Fontiveros. Although the remorseful uncle promised to improve the situation, Catalina didn't trust him. After a year away from home, Francisco returned to live with his mother and brothers. He was glad to be with them again, despite their meager surroundings. Unable to read or write, Francisco became a weaver, an occupation he would practice for the rest of his life.

Catalina struggled to put nourishing food on the table. A few years after Gonzalo's death, in the late 1540s, the middle son, Luis, became ill and died, probably from malnutrition. John would have been old enough to feel the loss.

John's physical condition could not have been good. Always small in stature, he probably suffered from rickets, a disease caused by poor nourishment. His most reliable early biographer, Jeronimo de San José, would later described him as being "between small and medium in height, well proportioned in body, although thin from the rigorous penance he performed."

Jeronimo also noted John's dark complexion and his becoming "venerably bald, with a little hair in the front" in later life. He had a broad forehead and dark eyes. John was robust enough to undertake tough trips over rugged landscapes.[4]

Despite their widely different ages, Francisco and John got along well. John was unlike other children in the town, many of them from larger families. John probably spent much time alone. Perhaps this solitude sharpened his focus on God, which only grew as he got older. Later in life, advocating the cultivation of prayerful solitude, John advised: "Be joyful and gladdened in your interior recollection with him [God], for you have him so close to you. Desire him there, adore him there."[5]

Relocating to Survive

Although Francisco was helping to bring money into the fatherless family, in about 1548 ongoing poverty led Catalina to move with her two surviving sons to Arevalo, eighteen miles northeast of Fontiveros. She must have felt heartbroken to leave the town where she and Gonzalo had met and where she buried him and their son. But she courageously undertook the trip, hoping to improve the family's lot.

Once settled in Arevalo, Catalina and Francisco found employment as day-laborers in weaving shops. The still thin but growing John went to school. He closely observed the comings and goings of his older brother, Francisco, who got involved in some time-wasting pranks and misdeeds. With the help of a priest who urged the older boy to turn toward better patterns of living, Francisco quieted down and began to practice calming prayer. He often sought niches outdoors in which to lie down and focus on God, and in tough weather he did so in church or at home. Who knows what impact this example of contemplative practice may have had on young John?

Eventually Francisco met and married Ana Izquierda, who filled out the small household with her presence. Along with Catalina, and though owning little, the newlyweds shared their goods with people more destitute than themselves. Sometimes they even sheltered the needy in their little home. This atmosphere of love and selfless care for the downtrodden certainly made its mark on John.

The Yepes household continued to struggle financially, and around 1551, when John was nine, Catalina decided to move the family once again, this time twenty miles northwest to Medina del Campo, the market town where Gonzalo had sold cloth. As was the case in their prior locations, the family lived in a predominantly Islamic neighborhood. This fact has led some historians to consider the possibility that the Catholic Catalina had at least some remote Muslim background.[6]

Medina del Campo came alive each year in the spring and fall. Vendors and customers of cloth thronged to its lively fairs. As experts in weaving, the Yepes family benefited from the yearly trade and decided to make Medina del Campo their permanent home. Here Catalina seized an opportunity to have John sent to a "catechism school," the School of Doctrine, recently established in Medina. The institution's purpose was to combat delinquency among young men of poor families. While staying there, not far from his family, John would have education and faith formation. He would work alongside artisans in order to earn his keep. John enrolled in the school around 1552. As Francisco would later tell it, his younger brother and the other students (aged seven to fourteen) were apprenticed to masters of assorted trades: carpentry, tailoring, wood-carving, and painting. Few students were expected to move on to further studies. Disappointingly, John did not gain enough proficiency in any of the trades, although his dabbling in them gave him the basic skills he would use throughout life. His awareness of tools and methods also gave the future poet examples and metaphors he could later employ when writing about matters far more sublime.

Despite his awkwardness in the skills of various trades, John had exceptional proficiency in language arts and handwriting. Run by Augustinian religious sisters, the school provided Catalina a lifeline in her heroic efforts to raise John. His studies readied him to tackle advanced subjects in an academic life that was rare and perhaps suspect among his illiterate family members and neighbors. Moreover, it richly supplied the boy with faith-based discipline adapted from a monastic model.

John was among those chosen from the school to assist most mornings with duties at La Magdalena, the local church with its attached convent. Serving Mass and running errands for the sisters gave John a sense of accomplishment he had not found in the manual trades. He enjoyed worshiping at Mass, and the Gospel message captivated him more than most of his peers. The sacristans and the Augustinian sisters acclaimed him for his intelligence, maturity, and virtue. He used these gifts when he was sent out into the streets to beg for the livelihood of the school. Accustomed to difficulty, John proved he could apply himself to this unappealing task. His steadiness and flexibility prepared him to serve in new and more challenging ways.

As with most young boys, John experienced calamities. He once fell into a well while playing, and the adults who had rushed to his aid were surprised he had not drowned. They threw him a rope and pulled him to safety, but John attributed his rescue mostly to the Blessed Virgin Mary's protection. Indeed he was full of religious fervor. He delighted in reading about the lives, feats, and miracles of the early Christian monks, which were available to him in highly sensationalized stories. The accounts fueled his sense of God's power at work in people open to letting God guide them.

Back at home, the Yepes family continued to face loss. Francisco and his wife, Ana, suffered the deaths of all but one of their seven or eight children.[7] Yet, despite his personal sorrows, the bereaved father spent much of his time begging for the poor. The civil authorities once suspected him of being a self-seeking nuisance until they discovered how much his begging helped the destitute. As he roamed the streets, Francisco often carried unfortunate people into the community's hospitals. At that time, abandoned infants were brought to church for adoption by welcoming families, and Francisco helped orchestrate that charitable process. Catalina once provided a home for a dying baby. The struggling Yepes family steadily resisted inevitable temptations toward bitterness or self-pity. Soon John would show that he had learned these lessons well.

CHAPTER TWO

Drawn Toward Service

Consistent with his family's dedication to relief work despite their own misery, John began serving as an attendant at Las Bubas, Medina del Campo's plague hospital. This institution primarily served poor, disgraced patients suffering from tumors (*las bubas*) caused by the sexually transmitted diseases that were spread by conquistadors returning from the New World. The hospital had fifty occupied beds in large, public wards. Relegated to the town's outskirts, it was viewed more as a holding place for dying outcasts than as a source of physical healing. John worked at Las Bubas under the direction of its altruistic administrator, Don Alonso Álvarez, who devoted his time and money to care for people who could never repay him. For the patients' welfare, John was sent to beg for funds among the town's market stalls and gatherings. Undoubtedly, he met rejection and indifference as he appealed to strangers to assist the patients he had come to know and compassionately treat. Having lived a hardscrabble existence himself, John's work among the dying intensified his awareness of people's sufferings. John tried to bring the patients some cheer by telling stories and singing songs he had heard from Francisco and around the city. His joy-filled attentiveness to patients' needs conveyed his respect for their inherent dignity. It also solidified his identity as a man of selfless service, willing to do anything needed. What John learned at Las Bubas benefited not only him but also the people he would later influence. Through this experience, John "was exposed to life's open wounds, and was formed by that exposure."[1]

Don Álvarez assessed John's potential and soon offered him the chance to embark on a path usually reserved for the children of rich families. He gave John the opportunity to take courses at Medina's recently founded Jesuit college. He would serve at the hospital and study during his free hours. For four years, 1559 to 1563, John learned Latin, rhetorical exposition, poetry, the humanities, and perhaps Greek. The college also emphasized moral instruction, an element not found in comparable schools. In these busy, decisive years, John's work and study undoubtedly contributed to his maturing in faith, wisdom, and character. After John's death, Francisco recalled that late one night Catalina found John ensconced in a room filled with firewood, studying by the light of a primitive oil lamp.[2] He experienced the night as a time for growth and precious solitude. His later poetry uses images of nighttime darkness that demands taking risks and of blazing logs that emit warmth and light.

John's reputation for virtue began to spread throughout his community. Before long, Don Álvarez proposed a vocational plan to John. He would sponsor John's studies to become a secular priest so that he could one day serve as the chaplain at Las Bubas. A Church career was accorded much respect in Spain at that time. For many poor young men, the opportunity for such status and security would have been hard to resist. If that prospect held any appeal for John, he did not allow it to capture his heart. Neither did other pursuits attract him, despite the urgings of people in the town to use his gifts in any of many fine occupations. This was not a matter of John doing only what he preferred but was his attempt to discover what God wanted for him. He was leaning toward entering consecrated religious life, and he knew that he should follow where God seemed to be leading him. He turned down Don Álvarez's offer.

John's experience with helping the sisters during his school days had given him a close connection to the sacrament of the Eucharist, which was regularly celebrated at the convent. John was edified as he observed the sisters' devotion as they attended Mass. The priesthood's strong link to the Eucharist may have enticed John to consider it as his lifelong commitment.

Many vocations came from the Jesuit college in John's hometown of Medina del Campo. In answering God's call, young people joined not only the Jesuits but also other religious orders, including the Dominicans, Franciscans, and Carmelites. As a student there, John must have been encouraged to consider religious life by their presence. John's dedication to Mary, as seen in his near-drowning experience, resonated with the Marian orientation of Carmel.

The Church in Spanish Society

The Church in Spain was flourishing. King Ferdinand and Queen Isabella had unified Spain largely by asserting the close connection between Church and state. They used a common profession of Catholicism as a means of politically uniting Spain. They set up the Spanish Inquisition, which at first had been organized to stave off the tendency of Jewish converts to revert to their old religious practices. Eventually it investigated any person or movement that seemed a threat to solid Catholic teaching and practice.

The royal couple forged a generally workable relationship with the popes of their time, but the Church was subservient to the throne. The royal efforts led to significant Church reform. King Ferdinand and Queen Isabella worked to improve the quality of pastoral ministry carried out by bishops and parish priests. Then the monarchs turned their attention to improving the fervor of the men and women who belonged to religious orders. Reforms were put in place in the way of life practiced by these groups, and this effort greatly succeeded.

Isabella died in 1504 and Ferdinand in 1516, but their reforms set the Church in Spain on a stable course. King Charles V ascended to the throne in 1516. When he abdicated in 1556, Spain's rule fell to his son, King Philip II. This sovereign strongly opposed any advance of Protestantism into Spain. He also showed strong interest in continuing efforts to reform the religious orders as a way of bolstering the Catholic faith against any threats from Protestantism.

Meeting the Carmelites

After finishing his studies in Medina del Campo, John was better educated than most young men who shared his poor background. He had made something of himself. Poverty and rejection had sharpened John's strong values. His devotion to God, sensitivity to people, hard work, and intelligence set him free to serve God and others in quiet but remarkable ways. Though small in stature, John was beginning to stand spiritually tall.

In 1560, when John was eighteen, a new monastery of Carmelite friars opened in Medina del Campo and the townspeople began to take notice. The friars brought with them an interesting history. The Carmelites had first come to Spain during the thirteenth century. By John's time Castile had approximately three convents of women and ten houses of men with a total of about 100 friars. Medina's Carmelites offered lectures to students and townsfolk alike. The extent of John's connection to this community is not clear, but he may have attended presentations or studied under a professor attached to it. Something of the Carmelite spirit would attract John toward their way of life. God filled John with a longing for the Carmelite way, with its strong emphases on devotion to Mary and contemplation: a quieter, less word-filled type of prayer than he would have found to be practiced in other communities.

John must have learned of the Carmelites' proud legacy from members of the order. Their late-twelfth-century founding in the Holy Land had been inspired by the example of the Church's earliest monks. During the first few Christian centuries, these men and women had sought out the desert and fringes of towns as places of prayer and spiritual growth. At first they were solitaries living an eremitical life, but they eventually started to band together for common prayer and mutual encouragement. In quiet and peace, they allowed God to transform their spirits and replace their selfishness with selfless love. Their choice of a celibate life allowed for a direct, undistracted focus on building their relationship with God.

The Carmelites emulated the centuries-earlier monastic flight into solitude. For the first sons of Carmel, that solitude was not literally in the desert but near a cool spring in the Holy Land. Gathering themselves into a religiously oriented federation of hermits, these anonymous pioneers settled in a ravine on the slopes of a range of hills jointly called Mount Carmel. That scenic range became the Carmelites' intentionally chosen equivalent of the classic desert setting.

The members lived in individual cells and desired to be "meditating day and night on the law of the Lord," as worded in their simply composed rule of life, *The Rule of Saint Albert*.[3] That rule did not mention any pastoral activity to those outside the community. In the midst of their cells, they built a small oratory, literally a place for prayer. They dedicated it to Mary under the title "Our Lady of Mount Carmel."[4] In keeping with the egalitarian caste of the group, Mary became something of a sister to the "Brothers of Our Lady of Mount Carmel," their more formal name. The friars (brothers) pledged obedience to God and to their superior. They held property in common, living simply so as to be unencumbered by whatever could distract them from knowing, loving, and serving God.

The Carmelite order evolved significantly after its foundation. Within a few decades, concern over the threat of Muslim aggression led many members to uproot themselves from their beloved Mount Carmel. Around 1235 the Carmelites returned to Europe and began to spread there. In their transition from their holy mountain to places throughout Europe, they persisted in their desire to retain vestiges of an eremitical life.

Meanwhile, by the Middle Ages Benedictine monasticism was flourishing in Europe. Well-organized monasteries had arisen throughout the Christian world. Though the monks and nuns lived simply, their institutions needed to be well rooted in the locale and prosperous enough to withstand the difficulties that could threaten a monastic community. Members could not therefore easily pick up and go wherever the Church's mission needed them. In the early 1200s Saint Francis and Saint Dominic established mendicant orders (from the Latin *mendicare*, to beg). The mendicant friars did not stay in one place but went about the countryside preaching wherever the Church needed them. Thus, the Carmelites, transplanted from the Holy Land to Europe, also began to follow a mendicant type of life. All mendicant groups valued equality among their members. Begging or working to sustain their basic needs, they strove to become truly poor in material goods as well as in spirit. The largest mendicant groups, such as the Franciscans, Dominicans, and Augustinians, maintained religious habits, prayed in common, and promised permanent commitment. They operated as "orders," congregations of disparately located members who lived not in one large community but in changeable, small groups. They lived as brothers to one another and to people they served. Their leaders were not abbots as in monasteries, but "priors" or "guardians," depending on the order. The following neatly summarizes the main characteristics of mendicant spirituality: "mobility in place of monastic stability, corporate as well as personal poverty, the following of modified monastic prayers and practices, and a commitment to pastoral ministry."[5] The key characteristics of medieval piety as found in the mendicants are: "devotion to the humanity of Christ; tender devotion to the Virgin Mary, Mother of Christ and therefore *Mater Misericordiae* (Mother of Mercy); devotion to the saints and angels; and the new cult of [devotion to] the 'Blessed Sacrament.'"[6]

When the Carmelites had left the Holy Land, they had remained free of property ownership to allow them to move in small groups to continue the mission of Christ. In view of its roots and subsequent movement, the Carmelite order tried to maintain its own distinctive complementary thrusts: the one more contemplative and the other more ministerially active.

Entrance into Carmel and Early Years as a Professed Religious

In 1563, at age twenty-one, John took a major step when he entered the Carmelite monastery of Santa Ana in Medina del Campo. He made this move secretly, probably since various religious orders had been enticing him to join. Soon after moving into the Carmelite house and receiving solid instruction in the basics of consecrated life and Carmelite traditions, he began to wear the habit and he received the name Brother John of Saint Matthias. John quickly advanced to the novitiate, a period of intense spiritual formation filled with silence and solitude. Then, in the summer of 1564, with the first year having progressed well, John professed his vows as a Carmelite. Besides his new community of brothers, the ceremony was attended by his friend Don Álvarez, and probably his mother, brother, and sister-in-law.

After his profession, Friar John requested and received permission to live as a Carmelite in a particularly austere way. He wanted to live according to the more primitive, stricter version of the Carmelite rule, as had been followed originally. In a sense, the simplicity of Carmel's heritage offered John the chance to stay consistent with his life since birth: a way of starkness and near-destitution but also self-donating love.

Right after his profession of vows, John left Medina del Campo and moved fifty-five miles southwest to the intriguing university city of Salamanca. The Carmelite house of prayer and studies, established in 1480 for Spaniards advancing in their preparation to live the Carmelite life forever, would be his base from 1564 to 1568. This house of less than a dozen Carmelite students was known for its strict discipline.[7] At the time, the respected University at Salamanca educated 7,000 young men, and its intellectual milieu provided the mainstay of an otherwise faded city filled with poor and often rowdy students.

Decades earlier, Cardinal Ximenez de Cisneros, known for his piety and verve as well as his toughness, had played an important role at the university. He worked closely with King Ferdinand and Queen Isabella and some churchmen to secure its place as a preeminent school of liberal arts. He also wanted to assist the reform of religious orders. In keeping with the latter aim, he strove to make devotional books available to both consecrated religious and ordinary folks. Many in Spain were exposed to a kind of prayer that led to a profound experience of God. John stood open to this kind of formation, not only as a Carmelite recruit but also because of his personal affinity.

Exceptionally qualified for academic life, John studied in Salamanca under leading experts in philosophy and theology. Living in Spain's Golden Age, John had the chance to explore the literature and language of his Spanish heritage. He became well prepared to mine these sources in his later writings. Logic, ethics, physics, astronomy, and politics held a strong place in the curriculum, but we do not know which courses he actually pursued. Religious studies in the university centered on Thomas Aquinas' theology of Jesus Christ and of the moral life, but also gave attention to a breadth of other theologians. With considerable debate, different academic outlooks vied to capture the students' loyalties. Staying out of the fray, John seems to have blended university study with classes in his order's house of studies. Living in the Carmelite students' house, he had quiet time for prayerful reflection on his professors' lessons and on the Carmelite heritage. His later writings indicate that he fully delved into the treasures of the wider Catholic spiritual tradition, either on his own or in classes. He explored the ideas of medieval theologians who emphasized not only understanding the ways of God but also having personal experience of God in a relationship termed mystical.

At Salamanca John wrote a report (now lost) to distinguish between the emerging and dangerous Illuminism of the *Alumbrados* and the Church's tried-and-true tradition regarding prayer and the spiritual life. The *Alumbrados* espoused a quiet and contemplative way of prayer, but dismissed vocal prayer and ascetic practices. They disparaged human efforts to cooperate with God's lead and devalued the use of images in prayer. Many of these Illuminists went so far as to reject the sacraments and Christian tradition. Against these extremists, John upheld the Church's tradition of respect for the three main ways of prayer: vocal, with words and thoughts; meditative, with consideration of ideas; and contemplative, savoring virtually without words the loving presence of God. Although John emphasized going deeper into the third type of prayer, he never advocated rejecting the other two, but valued combining ways of praying. As he would later advise: "Seek in reading and you will find in meditation; knock in [vocal] prayer and it will be opened to you in contemplation."[8] For John, "contemplation is nothing else than a secret and peaceful and loving inflow of God."[9]

The Spanish Inquisition had condemned the *Alumbrados*, but strains of their thinking remained during John's lifetime. This provoked unfortunate suspicion of valid ways of prayer that were quieter and more interior than standard recitation of formulaic prayers. With that, the Church's rich legacy of authentic mysticism was called into question. John kept his balance as he tried to help others maintain theirs. He valued meditation especially as a way to follow and imitate Christ. Still, he was eager to help people pray contemplatively.[10]

From his few years of pre-ordination studies, John advanced a view of the human person as created with the capacity to know and encounter God and to grow in greater union with him. This union would bring one to see life and people more as God sees them and to love them as God loves them. John's balanced sense of the human person would make him a competent spiritual director throughout his life.

Study of the Bible enthralled John. He had a deep familiarity with both the Old and the New Testaments. In particular, three Old Testament figures who had suffered but ultimately received God's consolation made a lasting impression on John. First, Job, whose painful deprivations eventually led him to a stronger relationship with God. Second, the prophet Jeremiah, who remained faithful to God despite strong opposition and his own limitations. And finally, King David, who praised his saving God despite his own weakness and the evil around him. Saint Gregory the Great's treatise on the Song of Songs also captured John's attention. With its story of a loving relationship between God the Creator and God's beloved, that Old Testament book became a lifelong favorite.[11] John also cherished the Gospel of John, continually pondering chapter 17, in which Jesus prays to his Father to keep his followers dedicated to what is truthful and loving amid life's challenges.[12]

It is widely thought that before his final year at Salamanca John was earmarked to become the prefect of studies in his Carmelite house. As prefect, he would review the course material for his fellow student-brothers. He would also be expected to enter into debate as well as to present and defend theses with theological rigor. This honor would suggest that John had proven himself a fine student and a responsible, respected brother in the community. By digging into the truths of his faith and asking questions without losing basic trust in God, John had learned that growth in faith often requires leaving behind the familiar and consoling. That insight would stay with John for a lifetime.

Rooted in Carmel's rich heritage and deep prayer, John was a model of dedication to Carmel. But even exemplary members of religious orders seldom make it to profession of vows without struggle. John was no exception as he discerned whether to continue on the Carmelite path. The competitive environment surrounding the university became repulsive to the sensitive young friar. He was accustomed to building others up rather than tearing them down. Perhaps he had become disenchanted with the striving for honors and recognition, "the point-scoring and one-upmanship of the university world."[13] He saw the dangers that this misleading motivation presented to students from religious orders, including the Carmelites. Fortunately for Carmel and the Church, John knew that knowledge and educational degrees do not guarantee happiness or holiness. With his scholarly talents and devotion to prayer, John may have found it hard to balance both aspects in his intense student life in Salamanca. He may well have feared that he might be assigned to academic work if he stayed in Carmel.[14]

Without causing a stir, John began to consider leaving the Carmelites and joining the much more austere Carthusians. He may have encountered Carthusian students in Salamanca. Early in John's stay at the Carmelite house of studies, the Carmelite Father Prior General Rossi (called Rubeo in Spain) had encouraged the young members to live the Carmelite way of life vigorously. John's relationships with his housemates may have shown him the gap existing between the Carmelite ideal and reality.

Tradition holds that John's peers found him overly serious and austere. His personal habits—studying hard, praying in solitude, fasting, and whipping himself as a form of penance—began to separate him from his fellow student Carmelites. If John offered suggestions or occasional fraternal corrections, this may have further distanced him from his confreres. He seemed to be excluded from the brotherly support that should characterize Carmelite communities. This would have been painful for him, with his sensitive disposition.[15] Perhaps John's perceptive nature suggested that he might not fit permanently in Carmel. Was God really calling him there? If not, then where?

Chapter Three

Meeting La Madre

Help would come to John in an unexpected way. A Carmelite nun, Sister Teresa of Jesus (Saint Teresa of Ávila), had decided to strike out boldly and establish a reformed convent of Carmelite nuns, a foundation that blossomed into the Carmelite Reform that would change the course of John's life as well.

Born in Ávila in 1515, Teresa de Cepeda y Ahumada was a very different person from John. Twenty-seven years older than he, she came from a financially comfortable family, had a gregarious personality, and had little formal education. Yet, in their commitments to loving God, praying deeply, and ending up living Carmelite life to the full, the two were quite similar.

Teresa: Reformer of Carmel

In 1535, at age twenty, Teresa had entered the local Carmelite convent, the Incarnation, at Ávila. The community was very large; its members came from varied social and economic backgrounds. Some had servants, while others had no such help. Sisters were free to come and go as they chose. Visits with the convent's benefactors, and with both male and female friends in the visitors' parlor or speakroom, were part of daily life. The vivacious Teresa got right into the swing of chatting with people who often came to visit.

Fortunately, while convalescing from a serious illness, Teresa became drawn more deeply into a way of prayer called "recollection," a method promoted mainly by some Franciscans. As explained in Francisco de Osuna's *Third Spiritual Alphabet*, published in 1527,[1] this prayer involved a process of emptying oneself, "thinking of nothing" so as to fix one's heart on God, who calls everyone to friendship and deeper communion with him.[2] Teresa enthusiastically began to practice this kind of prayer, but she eventually fell away from it and endured years of spiritual dryness and struggle. As Teresa described it, her life was marked by "this battle and conflict between friendship with God and friendship with the world."[3] She found herself "with these fallings and risings and this evil—since I fell again—and in a life so beneath perfection."[4]

After some remarkable experiences of conversion and the resulting growth in prayerful friendship with Christ, Teresa became convinced that the Carmelites needed to live their charism more radically. She noted the high standards of religious life promoted by Spain's King Philip II. The commitment of some Franciscans and other religious who were exploring the ideals of their founders also inspired her. Philip II strongly held that the dissolution of Christian unity, which had followed on the dissent of Martin Luther and others, stemmed largely from the failure of religious orders to live according to their ideals. Philip greatly feared that without a profound reform of its religious orders, Spain would fall prey to Protestantism and lose its national unity and prosperity.

In 1560, Teresa and a few of her fellow nuns at the Incarnation began to discuss the possibility of founding a new, reformed Carmelite convent in Ávila. They envisioned a Carmel that would closely follow the original rule and the eremitical, contemplative spirit of its beginnings. They dreamed of having time each day for quiet prayer, of each sister having equal status within the house, and of being freed from economic ties to certain noble families who were benefactors of the community. Such ties bound them to spend much time in wordy prayers for those patrons. If released from the undue influence of benefactors, the nuns could focus on core values: imitation of Christ and interior freedom. Maintaining a community of fewer members would enhance mutual support among them.[5]

Soon, Teresa requested and received permission to establish a house for Carmelite nuns dedicated to a reformed way of life. Amid controversy and some delays, Saint Joseph's monastery opened at Ávila, and Teresa became head of a community that included four novices.

Teresa had not envisioned opening new houses, but the Prior General of the Carmelites encouraged her to establish many other houses of the Reform. Teresa became the traveling foundress of sixteen more monasteries for women and ten for men. Now envisioning further expansion, she intended the communities to be mission-oriented in a specific sense: they would provide a powerhouse of prayer for all the works of the Church. Professing strong faith and praying fervently, the sisters would present an alternative to heresy, promote a remedy for the Church's internal weaknesses, and offer a model of holiness to the whole Church.[6]

In her efforts at reform, Teresa looked back at earlier historical attempts. The late Middle Ages, especially around the time of the Black Death in the fourteenth century, had witnessed a general decline in the religious observance of consecrated religious. For the Carmelites, this downward spiral was exacerbated in 1430 when Pope Eugene IV allowed a "mitigation" or lessening of the strictness of some aspects of the Carmelite rule. This action moved some Carmelites for decades afterward to demand a return to a more eremitical life.

The life and legacy of Prior General John Soreth, who served from 1451 to his death in 1471, allowed for solid reforms that touched many Carmelite houses. This reforming Carmelite composed a widely-read commentary on *The Rule of Saint Albert.* At that time, the Order had only friars and no nuns. In a decisive move, Soreth not only welcomed women into the Carmelite family as nuns but also began associations of lay persons as tertiaries or third-order members. After the nuns were first established in the Low Countries, they soon spread to Italy, France, and Spain. The reforms of Soreth and others in the fifteenth and early sixteenth centuries had some good effects. But those effects were often spotty and temporary. Teresa would do better, though it would mean a lot of hard work.

Teresa's Appealing Invitation

A few months after John's ordination in 1567, he returned to Medina del Campo to celebrate Mass with his family and friends. Teresa was visiting the city, planning to open a second house for her nuns. By this time, her superiors had permitted her to enlist Carmelite friars to extend the Reform. Teresa wanted the men of Carmel to follow the same spirit as in her reformed women's communities. She thought, however, that the men's houses should forego the strict enclosure practiced by the nuns because her superiors insisted that the friars publicly preach and teach the people. Teresa also longed for the assistance of the Carmelite friars in guiding the nuns in the ways of prayer and virtue.

Father Antonio de Heredia, prior of the Carmelite men's house in Medina, had already volunteered for the reformed life. Just like John, Father de Heredia told Teresa that he had recently considered transferring to the Carthusians. She appreciated his experience and accepted him, though she was wary of his reputation for ambition and vanity. Teresa kept looking for someone more promising to join him.

John visited Teresa at Medina on April 12, 1567. He was intrigued to meet *La Madre*, whose good reputation had been spreading. She painted for John an appealing picture of a sufficiently reformed Carmel: "communities small enough to be united, poor enough to be free, committed to seeking God's friendship in prayer, as a way of helping to heal a world 'on fire.'"[7]

Teresa was very impressed with her potential recruit, and she quickly understood John's vocational crisis. Later she expressed her esteem for him:

> And when I spoke with this young friar, he pleased me very much. I learned from him how he also wanted to go to the Carthusians. Telling him what I was attempting to do, I begged him to wait until the Lord would give us a monastery and pointed out the great good that would be accomplished if in his desire to improve he were to remain in his own order and that much greater service would be rendered to the Lord. He promised me he would remain as long as he wouldn't have to wait long.[8]

After their encounter, both their lives changed, but John had no inkling of the challenges Teresa's invitation would bring.

Teresa viewed John as an answer to her prayers. After he promised Teresa he would remain in Carmel, they must have felt great hope for the future. She said of him, "Although he is small, I know that he is great in the eyes of God."[9] With her penchant for humor, she called her first recruits, Antonio and John, "a friar and a half," referring either to John's small size or to her less-than-full endorsement of Antonio![10]

John found not only the prospect of the Reform appealing, but also Teresa's particular method. Being a peaceful man averse to conflict, he appreciated her approach of setting up new houses filled with willing participants rather than switching existing houses to a reform mode.

As had been planned, John returned to Salamanca for a year of post-ordination study in theology. As he thought about his future, he needed to trust that God was guiding him. He would later write: "If anyone is seeking God, the Beloved [God] is seeking that person much more."[11]

After his year at Salamanca, John was eager to begin a foundation of reformed Carmelite friars. Teresa, Father de Heredia, and John made plans for the two men to move to obscure Duruelo, a crossroads between Ávila and Salamanca. Near John's birthplace, it was seventy-eight miles east of Medina del Campo. Sight unseen, Teresa had arranged for a donated farmhouse to be their residence. Seeing it before the others, Teresa's heart sank at its broken-down condition. Still, she dared to tell the men that the house would be sufficient—even if barely. They submitted to her plans without murmuring. As Teresa related it, the eager Antonio told her "that he would be willing to live not only there but in a pigsty. Fray John of the Cross was of the same mind."[12]

While Father de Heredia was gathering materials for the future house, John spent time with Teresa, who wanted to instruct him. Ever on the go, Teresa suggested that John accompany her on a journey she had to make between Medina del Campo and the town of Valladolid, twenty-eight miles away. A new women's foundation was being established there. Thus the nun and the friar, with a few other associates, became travel companions during the summer of 1568. Thinking back on that time, Teresa wrote of John: "He was so good that I, at least, could have learned much more from him than he from me. Yet this is not what I did, but I taught him about the lifestyle of the sisters."[13]

During her tutorial for John, Teresa reinforced the way of recollection she had come to cherish and practice. As she saw it, God calls everyone to prayerful communion with him since he has created us all in his image. God wants to unite each person with himself, and in so doing God gradually transforms each person. Good works and public prayers are not the sum total of Christian living, although they are helps to it. The meeting of the soul with God happens in the person's deepest center. Thus, quiet, contemplative prayer is the important aim.[14] On this journey, something of Teresa's joy and common sense began to replace the overly strict manner of religious life John had displayed among his peers in Salamanca. After the sojourn, John came away convinced that his ongoing Carmelite commitment could be lived well. He had also learned a lot about the women's Carmelite Reform. It included time for leisurely recreation, something that Teresa wanted John to adapt to the men's Reform movement. Such elements may not have naturally appealed to him, but Teresa's sense of healthy Carmelite life freed him to trust her. Nevertheless, he was too principled to be silent about what he felt needed to be addressed, while a determined Teresa was unaccustomed to being opposed by close associates.[15] This led to some conflict. They tended, however, to differ not about essential matters but about ways of organizing the new life—sharing their deep dedication to God.[16] By enlisting John, Teresa assisted God in bringing new life to him, and through him to herself, Carmel, and the Church. As they continued working together, their efforts would bear fruit in some unexpected ways.

Chapter Four

• • • • • • • • • • • • •

Pioneering a New Way

In September 1568, John set out for Duruelo from Valladolid, accompanied by an essential helper, the sisters' stonemason. Since John would be arriving a few months ahead of Father de Heredia, his job was to make the dilapidated residence livable. Stopping in Ávila on the way, John carried a letter of introduction from Teresa to a hometown friend, Francisco de Salcedo. She had written in high praise of John:

> . . . although he is small, I know that he is great in the eyes of God. Certainly we will miss him much here, for he is wise, and just right for our way of life. I believe our Lord has called him to this task. There's not a friar who does not speak well of him, for he had been living a life of great penance, even though he is young. It seems the Lord is watching over him carefully, for although in trying to get everything settled we met with a number of troubles—and I myself must have caused trouble at times by becoming annoyed with him—we

> never saw an imperfection in him. He's courageous, but since he is alone, he needs all that our Lord gives him for taking this work so much to heart.[1]

Teresa trusted de Salcedo as a prudent man who had offered her sound spiritual advice many years before. In her letter, she asked de Salcedo to counsel John to moderate his tendency toward excessive penances. If de Salcedo did so, it seems to have had little impact on John.

Leaving Ávila, the young friar and the stonemason continued toward Duruelo. Wearing his shoes and the Carmelite habit of fine cloth, John changed along the way into a simpler and shorter habit of coarse material that Teresa and two of the sisters had fashioned. He also took off his shoes and walked barefoot, thus physically enacting the switch from being calced (shoe-wearing) to Discalced (without shoes), as his new way of Carmelite living would soon become known. The primitive Carmelite rule included the custom of not wearing shoes, and some Franciscans and others adopted this practice to express their radical commitment to God. It concretized the effort to be spiritually and materially poor, and to avoid any sense of being literally "well-heeled."[2]

Once John reached Duruelo, the hard work began. The dwelling was more of an abandoned storage building for wheat than a farmhouse, but he and the stonemason improved it according to the plans Teresa had laid out. John was happy to live in poverty in imitation of Jesus. John was convinced that all followers of Christ, Carmelites or not, needed to know Christ's life story in order to pray to him and take him as the model for their life. John once said, "I would not consider any spirituality worthwhile that wants to walk in sweetness and ease and run from the imitation of Christ."[3] Thus, John placed crosses and skulls—well-established artistic symbols of human mortality—inside and outside the house. For John these were symbols not only of Christ's death but also of resurrection to a life of joy and love. John carved many of the crosses. No passerby could fail to notice this building as one housing men who took seriously their commitment to God and to simple, holy living. Neighbors had been warned that the occupants were attempting a new experiment in Carmelite living, and the looks of the property intrigued them. The local people held to the culturally ingrained sense that a religious house of prayer and penance would bring spiritual strength to its surrounding community. Soon they came to affirm and learn from their new neighbors.[4]

John's brother, Francisco, joined him and helped to ready the house, but he also accompanied John on trips to the surrounding towns. John traveled to assist pastors with preaching, instructing, and hearing confessions—practices Teresa advocated. Whether Francisco liked it or not, his brother the simple friar habitually refused the grand meals offered by grateful penitents and others.

The active Carmelite community at Duruelo got its real start on November 28, 1568, when the provincial superior came for Mass. He brought with him the long-awaited Friar de Heredia. Other community members, probably two, also arrived, but little is known about them. To mark this important new beginning, John of Saint Matthias adapted his name to one Teresa had chosen for him: John of the Cross. Antonio de Heredia added "of Jesus" to his own name.

The start-up at Duruelo fulfilled the aspirations John had long harbored. Its establishment placed him squarely on a course of making his life's work the successful reform of Carmel. As Antonio de Nicolas has observed, John's work for the Reform

> was to be marked with the failures and successes of this mission. The failures were more visible than the successes, but seemed also to be directed to the deeper life Juan [John] was beginning to develop: the flight toward the solitary regions of mystical experience. He did not direct his efforts toward a political struggle with the outside world, as did Teresa de Ávila.[5]

The house was a joyful one, though poor and cramped. The men followed the primitive Carmelite rule, which stipulated that the community fast and abstain from meat between the feast of the Triumph of the Cross (September 14) and Easter. Daily John and his confreres practiced two hours of silent mental prayer. Intent on setting a pattern of frequent prayer, he introduced a practice not a part of the nuns' Reform: rising at midnight to pray the breviary in common. The friars also experienced joyful fraternal support and interaction with appreciative friends; many visited the house for confession. These people often gave their Carmelite neighbors bread and other supplies. Potential recruits came to see if they were called to that life, and a good number joined. One frequent visitor, Julian of Ávila, who traveled there regularly on foot for some retreat days, felt so inspired by the fervor of the little band of Carmelites that he thought of the place as a touch of paradise.[6]

In Lent of 1569, Teresa paid a surprise visit to Duruelo. She brought with her the memory of just how bare the property had been when she first eyed it. Now she saw it alive with Carmelite life. She was mostly reassured, but she noted its limitations:

> The choir was in the loft. In the middle of the loft the ceiling was high enough to allow for the recitation of the Hours, but one had to stoop low in order to enter and to hear Mass. There were in the two corners facing the church two little hermitages, where one could do no more than either lie down or sit. Both were filled with hay because the place was very cold, and the roof almost touched one's head.[7]

Teresa's one word of caution, spoken in her direct style, concerned the strictness of their lifestyle. As she later wrote, "after conversing with those Fathers, I spoke of some things and begged them especially . . . not to be so rigorous in penitential practices, for what they were doing was severe."[8] As much as Teresa promoted the simple life of a reformed Carmel, she wisely knew that the men needed to be living in well-equipped surroundings conducive to reading and study. For example, they needed to change their practice of going barefoot in the winter.[9] They took her advice, for Teresa was persuasive! After all, she had high hopes that those earliest Discalced friars would serve as leaders in Carmel for a long time.

Never one to prevent a good venture from expanding, Teresa eagerly saw to the founding of an additional men's Discalced community in Pastrana. That undertaking began somewhat hurriedly in the summer of 1569.

Expanding to Mancero de Abajo

Word soon came to the Duruelo community that a new, better location was available in Mancero de Abajo, 100 miles west of

Duruelo. When Friar de Heredia went to inspect it, he knew it would be more suitable for the twenty residents of the crowded Duruelo house. A wealthy, devout man had offered to construct a simple but more spacious building. The grateful community moved there in June 1570. However, the new location had no well for water. When an attempt to dig proved so successful that the water threatened to flood the yard and enter the house, Friar de Heredia was led to pray spontaneously, "Lord, we asked for water but not for so much."[10]

The community appreciated Mancero's advantages, but they felt a certain longing for Duruelo. They cherished it as their Bethlehem and returned to pray at the site from time to time.

John was becoming an experienced spiritual guide and, once settled at Mancero, was asked to travel to the other community in Pastrana. He took with him one of the Duruelo-Mancero novices, Friar Pedro, who later recalled how inspiring it was to accompany John on foot the whole way. As they traveled, they begged alms, gave what they received to the poor they met, and conversed about God. If offered a comfortable place to stay, John would graciously refuse the offer in favor of something simpler. John wrote on little slips of paper short sayings or maxims that expressed spiritual wisdom, and he gave these to Friar Pedro as they traveled together and spoke of many things. A contemporary described John in this way: "His bearing and conversation were peaceful, very spiritual and full of profit for those who listened to and talked with him."[11] The foundation in Pastrana housed fifteen men, both professed and novices. During the month he was there, John organized a novitiate program for the new members.

How gratifying it must have been for John to see his and Teresa's dream achieved: to lead others into the simple richness of a contemplative approach to the men's Carmel. After finishing his work in Pastrana, John returned to Mancero, which had become his home and where he would have been happy to remain. But his quiet life there would soon end.

On to the College Town of Alcalá de Henares

Having gained a reputation as a wonderful spiritual counselor, in April 1571 John was assigned to an important new task, which sprang from the hope that the men's Reform would continue attracting many recruits. John became the rector of a college for Carmelites joined with the university in Alcalá de Henares, near Madrid. John must have drawn on his own experience as a student-friar at Salamanca to assist the students. His watchword for them expressed his own approach to the studies he had excelled in: "A religious and a student; but a religious first, then a student."[12] Although a few of the men found John too demanding, many more commended him. Local men began to consider vocations to the Discalced Carmelites.

A young priest, Jerome Gracián, showed interest in the Carmelites while he was a student at the University of Alcalá. Three years younger than John, Gracián had been ordained a diocesan priest in 1569 or 1570 after studying at Madrid with the Jesuits. He moved to Alcalá de Henares to enter a program leading to a doctorate in theology and became impressed with the witness of the Carmelites in that university town. He entered the Reformed Carmel, where his story was to intertwine with

John's in a few different and sometimes troubling ways. Full of eagerness, Gracián began his Carmelite life in the Reform's second male foundation at Pastrana, during a rough patch in its young history.

Every human endeavor, including any undertaken for God, is prone to go off-track if the right principles are not followed. Teresa and the Carmelite leaders had chosen Friar Angel de San Gabriel to serve as the new novice master for the Pastrana community. However, he soon proved inept. Teresa described him as "a very young friar . . . who had no learning, very little talent, and no prudence for governing."[13] Teresa was regularly consulted about key appointments involving friars of the Reform, but she and the Carmelite leaders had only a few men whom Teresa would have trusted as superior of the Pastrana community. Though filled with youthful idealism, Friar Angel de San Gabriel was inexperienced and had a penchant for the dramatic. He had come under the influence of an overly rigorous Discalced Carmelite nun, Sister Catalina de Cordova. She had introduced extreme asceticism, stringent bodily penances, and an overly eremitical lifestyle to the convent she led. Friar Angel de San Gabriel's allegiance to her ways was coupled with a strange emphasis on parading ascetical practices before the townspeople. All this started to tip the balance of a solid religious life for the impressionable group of eager young men in formation. Indeed, if nothing were done to steer things rightly, many of the best recruits would leave Carmel.[14] At a critical time when the new Reform movement counted on building wide support, some of the townspeople were beginning to mock and dislike the friars. A quick change in leadership had to be made for the men of

Pastrana, and John temporarily became that house's rector. This occurred in early 1572, soon after his move to Alcalá.

The challenge John faced at Pastrana was rooted in a long-standing tension within Carmel. The order had been founded with a strong eremitical thrust, but also with provision for supportive, prayerful community life. The Carmelites had to give up some time and energy for these cherished elements when they adapted to a more active, mendicant lifestyle. At its best, the Carmelite tradition tried to hold three features in a life-giving combination: silence and solitude in God's presence, Christian community with one another, and active service of God's people. The Reform had a real appreciation for the dimension of service but subordinated it to the first aspect. Some of the men attracted to the Pastrana Carmel had ventured there specifically because of its penitential lifestyle. A few of them had been hermits affected by a recent Church law that obliged solitaries to become part of a recognized religious community. Many of these former solitaries were not disposed to grasp the importance of blending the elements of silence, community, and service. In particular, they found it difficult to focus their sense of the eremitical life on prayer rather than spiritual rigors. Other men, like Gracián, who joined the community at or near the time of John's brief service there, favored a more balanced approach to Carmelite life.

John had a lot to offer the friars of Pastrana. He knew that they needed to develop a deep desire for God, to whom they could open their minds and hearts in prayer. For John, "[t]he desire for God is the preparation for union with him."[15] After all, John had also learned from Teresa to forego excessive penances in favor of reflective prayer.

Reform often leads to protest, and so it was for John. The master of novices at Pastrana soon wrote to Teresa to complain about John's priorities. With her healthy knack for consulting others in disputed matters, Teresa sent the letter to her confessor and confidante. He replied to affirm and vindicate John, whose work at Pastrana soon proved somewhat successful. Teresa's confessor knew and communicated forthrightly what John had come to see ever more clearly: that penitence is not an end in itself, but rather a route toward growth in spiritual life.[16]

As things returned to normal at Pastrana, John happily returned to the house of studies in Alcalá. Though Gracián was new to Carmel, he became invaluable at Pastrana for his gentleness, intelligence, charm, and charisma. Teresa found in him, as she had in John, someone who inspired confidence. In fact, something about Gracián impressed Teresa in ways that John could not quite match. Gracián was surely more of a go-getter, having come to Carmel from a prominent political family in which he had learned to deal deftly with people in positions of authority. Gracián had never been prone to excessive penances and seemed to thrive on interacting with people. He and John were two different men. While John preferred prayer and a more properly spiritual ministry,[17] Gracián had a more actively ministerial inclination.

A Daunting Task at Ávila

John's stable situation in Alcalá de Henares was not to last long. Teresa had been named prioress of the Incarnation monastery in Ávila. This was the community she had first entered and later left to begin the Reform. Her move back to Ávila would soon affect John.

What accounted for Teresa's appointment to the unreformed house she had voluntarily left? Her Reform had certainly been met with opposition at the Incarnation. Now relations between the two groups of Spanish Carmelites, Teresa's Discalced and the "observants" or "calced," were becoming even more strained. King Philip II supported Teresa's project, since he desired to continue Ferdinand and Isabella's thrust of reforming religious orders. He secured the right to appoint overseers, called "visitators," of mendicant orders' reform efforts. He boldly set in place a system whereby a local bishop would assign a reform-minded visitator to oversee religious orders in Spain. While this held promise for Teresa and her Reform, it was clearly awkward for the internal relations of religious orders. The major superiors of the Carmelites, based in Italy, feared their authority would be compromised if shared too widely. Likewise, the larger body of unreformed Carmelites worried that the smaller Discalced group was being favored. Grasping the tension, the enterprising King Philip wanted the visitator for the Carmelites in each Spanish region to be a Dominican, not a Carmelite. So it happened that the visitator for Castile, the Dominican Pedro Fernandez, could make major decisions, including the assignment of local superiors, such as Teresa. As much as Teresa and the Reformed Carmelites felt hopeful due to the backing of King Philip II and his appointees, they still came under the authority of the Rome-based Carmelite's Prior General Rubeo. Though his directives approved of Teresa's vision, they did not always coincide with the king's wishes for the Reform. The delicate situation was complicated because the Carmelite higher-ups and the king tried to convince the pope, who appointed a nuncio for Spain, of their viewpoint. A conflict of authority involving the Carmelite Prior General, the king, and the pope emerged. And Teresa, John, and the Discalced were caught in the middle of it.

Teresa's assignment to the Incarnation disheartened her. The visitator, Fernandez, intended the appointment to achieve a gradual infiltration of her vision into the monastery, like yeast in dough. But she was not convinced that a good result would occur. Foreseeing opposition to her appointment, she tried to dissuade Fernandez, but to no avail. Indeed, the day of Teresa's entry brought strongly expressed resistance within the house and the city. In fact, a riot ensued in Ávila as Teresa was installed as prioress.

As Teresa could have predicted, the Carmelite community was in financial trouble and the sisters needed generous friends to help fund the house. Always clever, she realized that the house had to be sustained, and thus that opposition within the city must not grow. Looking for spiritual support, she invited some Discalced friars to serve the nuns. For the crucial role of confessor for the large community, she chose John of the Cross. She trusted that he could eventually win over the Incarnation's Carmelite nuns opposed to the Reform. Convinced that his holiness would draw them, she also knew that an atmosphere of good feeling would keep the convent well regarded and solvent.

What Teresa wanted, she got. Before long, in May 1572, John left his important work at Alcalá for the challenging appointment in Ávila. In accord with the visitator's plan to combine Discalced and observant Carmelites, John moved into the friars' community in Ávila, located near the Incarnation. A few other Discalced friars had recently been transferred there and, in a controversial and awkward move, most of these men were given the highest positions in the community. John and one other friar served the nuns daily as confessors. The nuns who trusted Teresa must have found her endorsement of John reassuring: "I am bringing as your confessor a father who is a saint."[18] In view of how things eventually turned out, martyr would almost have been a more appropriate term.

John, a docile man of dialogue, learned a lot about spiritual growth from the nuns. In particular, he conversed with Teresa often during the time they spent together on the Incarnation's grounds. Each helped the other to make spiritual progress. Based on this time in their lives, some artists have depicted Teresa and John facing each other, speaking of God and drawn into ecstatic prayer. Teresa benefitted from John's education and wisdom, while he drew on her life-experience and hard-won progress in prayer. It was during this time that God gave Teresa the privilege of being in what she, John, and other mystics have called the state of spiritual marriage, a near-complete union with God in prayer. On November 18, 1572, as Teresa received Holy Communion from John, she experienced this spiritual marriage with Christ, the bridegroom of her soul.[19] Christ showed her the nail in his hand and told her to behold the nail, which he called a sign that someday Teresa would be his spouse.

About a year later, in mid-1573, John and his fellow Discalced confessor moved into a modest house on the property of the Incarnation.[20] Unsurprisingly, the sisters of the community, who had been accustomed to spending a lot of time in the speakroom meeting, entertaining, and hosting benefactors, at first met John's calls to greater solitude with considerable opposition. As John once said, "God does not fit in an occupied heart,"[21] but many of the nuns were occupied with all kinds of activities. Gradually, however, he won the esteem of many of the nuns. Sisters came to meet with him more willingly, and his days soon grew fuller as the community members grew holier. As they confessed to John and consulted with him, he would listen to them kindly and guide them firmly toward greater faith and charity. He directed the nuns to be attentive to what he would explain years later in a letter: "Keep this in mind, daughters: the soul that is quick to turn to speaking and conversing is slow to turn to God."[22] Before long, virtue was firmly rooted and the nuns knew John was on their side in their quest to grow closer to the Lord. To prod them on he again began to hand out pieces of paper with his brief sayings. His words and recommended prayer methods served as a breath of fresh air for those who had never had such resources.

In a few recorded instances, John's efforts helped to bring new perspectives on life—and sometimes new clothes!—to needy people in and beyond the monastery. When one sister had no shoes, John went into the city and begged for a pair for her to wear. When another sister lay dying, John kept a prayerful vigil with her and some of the sisters. He became their friend, and helped the Reform to advance there.

Nearby residents heard of John's reputation within the monastery, his visits to the sick and spiritually troubled, and his friendliness to those who came to consult with him. People knew he was holy and zealous, even if not everyone heeded his calls to embrace prayerful ways and to turn away from spiritually deadening practices.

In a few cases, puzzling events unfolded. One of the sisters in Ávila credited John with helping her resist the sexual advances of a man who came to visit her in the speakroom. Soon afterward, that man angrily confronted John and physically attacked him in the dark of night. In another instance, a woman who had been coming to the monastery to visit with John began to entice him inappropriately. John found her very attractive, but he mustered the strength he needed to stay chaste and to speak firm words to her. At another time, Augustinian superiors asked him to meet with one of their sisters, reputedly possessed by the devil. John found himself challenged to discover what was happening to her, but he consistently and calmly prayed for her deliverance. When she fully recovered, his reputation as an exorcist spread among Ávila's townspeople, and people sought him out for similar cases. He learned to distinguish between torments connected to spiritual warfare and those caused by mental illness. He had honed his skills as a spiritual guide.

At times, the Reform-related tensions within the Carmelites boiled over and burned John, who was the willing pioneer of the men's Reform. An example of this occurred when, in 1574, John accompanied Teresa to Segovia on one of her trips to undertake a new foundation. She knew she could count on John for instructing the nuns there on the spiritual life. They wanted to put their new house on firm footing. But Teresa had not obtained the proper permission from local Church authorities for the new convent. During the celebration of the inaugural Mass in the chapel, the vicar general of the diocese paid an unexpected visit. For proper protocols not being in place, John received a vehement but undeserved scolding!

While John resided near Teresa at the Incarnation, she was composing her *Foundations*, a compilation of her adventures setting up various houses of the Reform. Once she completed that work, she set her sights on writing her masterpiece, *The Interior Castle*. As the mature expression of Teresa's thoughts on prayer, which substantially flowed from her conversations with John, it is a practical guide to growth in prayer and holiness, and is filled with insights based on her own and others' experiences. The castle is a metaphor for the human person who advances toward its innermost room. That room signifies spiritual marriage: near-complete union with God and a truly authentic human existence. God dwells in that central space within this crystal castle. His shining love enlightens the path the person follows through its seven progressive mansions or apartments, each standing for a kind of prayer: from vocal to contemplative. One enters the most exterior room of the castle by resolving to pray faithfully and letting go of whatever attachments block the movement toward love for God. For Teresa, prayer was not merely saying prayers. Her helpful definition of prayer guided her sisters and, no doubt, also John: "For mental prayer in my opinion is nothing else than an intimate sharing between friends; it means taking time frequently to be alone with him who we know loves us."[23] On the human level, Teresa conversed regularly with friends, John certainly being foremost among them. For Teresa, prayer is a loving dialogue with God as friend.

While at the Incarnation, John of the Cross revealed his artistic talent in a few ways. For instance, he drew a sketch of

Jesus on the cross. Its perspective, intriguingly unusual, showed the Son seen through the eyes of God the Father looking down from heaven. The work later became the inspiration for other scenes with similar views, such as the twentieth-century artist Salvador Dalí's depiction of the crucifixion. John also sketched a drawing, akin to a chart, of the way a Christian would make spiritual progress in a figurative ascent to Mount Carmel's summit. In a different artistic expression, the nuns of the Incarnation worked with John to compose joyful poems about union with God.

In October 1574, Teresa's term at the Incarnation ended and she moved on from Ávila. By that time, however, John was a well-established presence among the sisters there. Although he had been brought to Ávila under difficult circumstances, in many ways his stay had proved life-giving for John and the nuns, including many who had been wary at first. He might have continued to prosper at Ávila, but tensions began to grow there as in Carmelite foundations throughout Spain. John was about to leave Ávila, but not by an ordinary transfer.

Chapter Five

A Prisoner Transformed

The cross was to prove an apt symbol for John during the rest of his life. Trouble had been brewing from afar during his happy, fruitful years at the Incarnation. The reform of both men's and women's branches had caused controversy. It was inevitable that certain factors would amass and clamp down on the Carmelite Reform and on John, who gradually was drawn into the disturbance. The various authorities who wanted to steer the Reform maintained clashing perspectives. This, joined to a breakdown in communication, soon led to trouble.

In August 1574, a new pope, Gregory XIII, bolstered the authority of the Carmelite Prior General Rubeo and his delegates to direct the affairs of Carmel and the progress of its reform. King Philip II grew angry that, without consulting him, the pope had acted to end the king's oversight of mendicant religious orders by means of visitators. Therefore, he declared the pope's ruling null on account of that deficiency.

Although Father Rubeo had once supported Teresa, he had grown cooler toward the Reform. He wrote two letters to Teresa (October 1574; January 1575), in which he asked her to share her sense of the conflicts among Spanish Carmelites. Apparently, Teresa did not receive his letters until June 1575. By May Rubeo had already convened a general chapter of the Carmelites in Piacenza, Italy. The large-scale gathering met to enact regulations for all Carmelites. Perturbed by Teresa's perceived resistance, Rubeo was disposed to protect the interests of the order's unreformed members (observants or calced). The Piacenza chapter attempted to maintain the order's unity by restricting the Discalced from growing in power.

Unfortunately, prior to the 1575 general chapter, the Andalusian visitator and Reform sympathizer, the Dominican Francisco Vargas, had overstepped his authority by establishing new Reformed houses in his region. That tipped the balance of power between the two Carmelite groups, resulting in negative ramifications for all the Reformed, including those in John's region of Castile, north of Andalusia.

Thus, the general chapter had been influenced by an anti-Reform reaction, one not softened by what many Carmelites, especially the observants, viewed as maverick moves by Vargas. The non-reformed Carmelites were also troubled by credible reports about the poor leadership among Discalced priors, such as Pastrana's prior from 1572, whose negative impact John had been called to reverse. That is why the chapter held in Piacenza decreed that no further Reform foundations be established and that Teresa confine herself and her Reform to just one house of her choosing. The future of the men's Reform was much threatened. Any appointments judged to have been made without the approval of proper Carmelite authorities were ended, placing John's position in Ávila in dispute.

A drastic event soon occurred—one that hinted at worse to come. In December 1575, the calced or observant prior of the men's Carmel in Ávila arrested John and his fellow Discalced friar at the Incarnation. They were transported to a jail-like section of the men's Carmelite monastery in Medina del Campo. This act expressed the resentment felt for the considerable influence John and his colleague wielded with the nuns at the Incarnation. Fortunately, relief soon came for John. Father Nicholas Ormaneto, the Reform-sympathizing papal nuncio in Spain, ordered the swift return of the two friars to the Incarnation and stipulated that only Discalced friars should be confessors for the sisters there. That relief would be short-lived, however.

To enforce its directives and to keep the Reform under strict control, the chapter at Piacenza dispatched its representative, Friar Jerome Tostado, to Spain. He was expected to be harsh toward the Discalced, and indeed he challenged both King Philip II and Father Ormaneto.

Pursued for Punishment

In late 1576, the Discalced friars of Andalusia held a chapter at Almodavar to fine-tune aspects of their life. As papal nuncio, Ormaneto had overseen the appointment of Friar Jerome Gracián as vicar general for Andalusia. Gracián initiated a move, backed by Teresa, to create a separate province for the Discalced. But his attempt did not succeed. At that meeting, with the Discalced so engrossed in discussing political strategies, John shared his views on some disputed issues. Even more, he spoke out boldly on the need always to develop their prayerfulness. Then John and the other attendees decided that he should step down as confessor at the Incarnation as a way of easing tensions with the calced friars. That didn't happen. The nuns at the Incarnation protested the idea. The Prior General wanted the Discalced friars to leave their ministry at the Incarnation, but the nuncio approved of John and his Discalced colleagues' service there. These mixed signals would lead to greater conflict.

The underlying tension between the reformed and unreformed members of the Carmelites of Spain reached a head when Ormaneto died suddenly in June 1577. The new nuncio, Felipe Sega, was far less sympathetic to the Reform. The crackdown on the Discalced Carmelite movement gained energy.

Against a background of jurisdictional conflicts rooted in basic disagreement as to the rightness of the Discalced Carmelite Reform, a dispute arose in October 1577. It concerned the election of a new prioress for the sisters at the Incarnation—with dire consequences for John. Eager to welcome back Teresa as their prioress, most of the ninety-eight nuns voted to elect her. But they did so against directives from higher Carmelite authorities. Ultimately, facing opposition for their stance, the nuns settled on another sister to lead them. Father Tostado thought that John and his companion at the Incarnation, Friar German, had influenced the sisters' pro-Teresa stance.

Taken to Toledo

With the tide turning against the Reform, power had shifted to those in favor of disbanding the Discalced men's way of life. Father Tostado soon demanded that John and German, whom the nuncio viewed as intruders, leave the Incarnation. In a conscientious reply, the two stated that they ought not to leave, for they were convinced that they had been appointed by proper authority. While John might have expected further dialogue on the matter, he could not have anticipated what would follow.

Less than two months after the nuns' election, during the night of December 3 and 4, 1577, members of the calced/observant Carmelite friars whisked Friars John and German from their rooms on the Incarnation's property. Tostado ordered the two men to be kept in separate men's calced Carmelite monasteries, to be housed in virtual jails. German was incarcerated in a nearby monastery in Ávila, but John was slated for a longer and harsher trip. Blindfolded and brutally escorted, a roundabout route was taken to disorient the captive. John had no idea where his final destination lay.

After traveling a few days, John arrived at the large men's Carmel in Toledo, where he would be imprisoned by the unreformed of his order for almost eight months. Looking back on his captivity, John drew comparisons to the Old Testament story of Jonah and termed his siege to be the time "after that whale swallowed me up and vomited me out on this alien port."[1]

Just two days after John's kidnapping, Teresa wrote to King Philip II asking for his help. Her letter indicates both her worry and some sarcasm:

> [Hernando Maldonado, the prior of the monastery in Toledo, is] holding these confessors captive in his monastery after having forced his way into their cells and confiscating their papers. The whole city is truly scandalized. He is not a prelate nor did he show any evidence of the authority on which these things were done. . . . Those friars [Maldonado and his men] dared so much, even though this city is so close to where your Majesty resides, that it doesn't seem they fear either justice or God. . . . I would consider the confessors better off if they were held by the Moors [the Muslims who had conquered Spain], who perhaps would show more compassion.[2]

Soon after reaching Toledo, John appeared before the monastery's superiors, opponents of the Reform. They subjected him to three successive pressure tactics: a demand for obedience, an offer of allurements, and a threat of punishment. Concerning the demand for obedience, John was aware of the longstanding official approval of the Discalced lifestyle, and he declined to relent in his faithfulness to the way of the Reform. The allurements might have changed the mind of a less dedicated friar: a promised appointment as a prior, the assurance of a well-outfitted cell and personal library, and the gift of a gold cross. John easily and resolutely rejected these offers. Not even the threat of punishment induced him to give in. In fact, he argued that the previous papal nuncio, Ormaneto, had supported his service at the Incarnation in Ávila, and that the approval by the royally appointed visitator, Fernandez, still deserved respect. Refusing to surrender, John was soon moved from a holding cell to a far less comfortable room. It did not help John at all when, back in Ávila, Friar German escaped from his confinement.

In Toledo's Carmelite monastery, John had to adapt to a complete change in lifestyle. Formerly he had enjoyed an active, fulfilling service as a spiritual guide. Now he was relegated to a virtual prison cell. His tiny room, once used as a latrine, measured only fifty to sixty square feet and had minimal daylight peeking in from a tiny opening high on one wall. He never received a change of clothing. His scapular and cowl, signs of his dignity as a Carmelite in good standing, were taken from him, and he was whipped regularly.

Some members of the Toledo community maintained great respect for John. They had known him in Salamanca during his student days, and they were kind to this prisoner in their midst. Others, however, blamed him for dividing the male Carmelite community in Spain, and they treated him disdainfully.

The friar appointed as John's jailer occasionally led him to an adjoining corridor for some exercise. The prisoner was allowed only one book, his copy of the breviary, and he was provided a bench on which to sit and pray with it. At certain times, he was led to the dining room, where he sat on the floor, separated from the other friars. No matter what a confrere might have thought of John, each was expected to administer the "circular discipline"—the community gathering in a circle and each member striking John's shoulders with tree branches. His meager diet hardly sustained him, and he was forced to fast from all food three days a week. Climate and air quality were consistently poor.

What are we to think of how the Carmelites treated one of their own? With charity, John later reflected that his misguided superiors had acted out of honest intentions to keep order and maintain what they saw as the good of Carmel. Indeed, monastery prisons had been established long before John's confinement. Communities needed ways of dealing with what was considered the wayward, disruptive behavior of members. Obviously, such means could be badly misused, as they were in John's case. Nowadays, the idea of friars being confined to an in-house jail cell is repulsive. We should remember, however, that in civil and Church government of the time, such prisons were common. The expectation was that each jurisdiction within society resolved its own need to correct and punish its citizens. That approach carried over to religious congregations, which exercised power over their own members. In fact, Teresa's Reform, when it later achieved an officially approved constitution, provided for jailing as a matter of necessity. Lawbreakers were handled internally, without exposing the conforming members to the feared evils of the troublemaker. Then, as now, sometimes exemplary people suffered misjudgment. John was certainly one of them, but his supposed misdeeds reveal the terribly complicated jurisdictional dispute.

While John remained imprisoned, his friend Teresa continued to try to influence authorities, all the way up to the king, to release him, but to no avail. She asked many people to pray for his liberation. Those prayers eventually were answered, but she probably could not have predicted the way John would find freedom—physically and spiritually.

The personal desperation John began to feel was worse than the harsh physical conditions he endured. His captors toyed with his emotions by telling him untruths about the Reform's decline. Naturally, this contributed to his feeling abandoned by those among whom he had vowed to live as a brother. He began to question seriously where he stood with God, to whom he had permanently committed his life in Carmel.

Although there seemed no escaping his sentence to physical darkness, something stupendous happened. John's confinement proved a decisive moment in his journey with God. His deprivation and desolation could have depleted his spirit and embittered him. But, brought low, John opened himself to God's power in his life. Detached from virtually all other supports, he disposed himself to being filled with God's powerful presence. God strengthened and deepened John's spirit. His confinement liberated him to know and love God even more. In his cell, John fell into deeper intimacy with his God, on whose friendship he so much needed to draw. By the end of his incarceration, John had grown spiritually. In the midst of the human harshness he witnessed, John's awareness of the innocent, life-giving sufferings of Christ crucified led him to a profound trust that divine action was more forcefully at work. John experienced his eight months in the dreary confines as a dark night masking the onset of a new dawn. The bleakness of his sentence was only the backdrop to John's deeper focus on God and on closer friendship with Christ. The three theological virtues of faith, hope, and love, poured into John (and all Christians) at Baptism, welled up within him. John interpreted his sufferings through the perspective of his faith. He resisted despair by maintaining hope, and he responded to cruelty with love. As we will soon see, filled with this hope, John sought a workable deliverance from his plight. The Old Testament Song of Songs helped John especially. In it is told the story of a lover who painfully experiences the absence of his beloved and is filled with a deep longing for union. Perhaps John was looking back on this dark period through which the light of God shone when he later offered this reflection: "Now that the face of evil more and more bares itself, so does the Lord bare his treasures the more."[3]

John had two jailers during his monastic imprisonment. A tough friar held this role from December 1577 to May 1578. Perhaps he treated John harshly because he would have been penalized for being too mild. Later he was replaced by a younger friar, Juan de Santa Maria, who was more naturally sympathetic. Apparently, without the permission of his superiors, the new jailer allowed John previously unknown liberties, including longer periods outside his cell. Juan de Santa Maria generously supplied John with paper, pen, and ink—useful for a great thinker and a man of prayer such as John. Decades later, in interviews conducted for John's beatification process, Juan de Santa Maria attested to the extreme tranquility, kindness, and gratitude John the prisoner had shown him. Viewing the disgraced John up close, this friar had detected God's saving work in him.

In Friar Juan de Santa Maria's words:

> During the time I was in charge, which was the latter part of his imprisonment, they brought him to the refectory three or four times, with all friars present, to receive the discipline, which they gave him with a certain severity. He never spoke, but rather bore it with patience and love. When this was over, they sent him back at once to his prison. Seeing his great patience, I felt compassion, and sometimes I opened the prison door after dinner and let him leave to get some air in a room across from the little prison.[4]

Toward the end of his confinement, John gave this second jailer two very personal gifts from the little he owned: a small crucifix and his breviary. Friar Juan de Santa Maria cherished the crucifix for the rest of his life.

John did not waste time in his cell. Rather, he prayed, using his breviary and his mental agility to recall from his considerable memory any biblical insights, words, songs, and stories he could dredge up. This inspired him to write some of the most important pieces of religious poetry our world has known: the first thirty-one stanzas of his *Spiritual Canticle*, *The Romances,* and *Stanzas of the Soul That Rejoices in Knowing God Through Faith*. For a person to come away from a great trial with fuller freedom, self-knowledge, prayerful intimacy with God (and in John's case, humility and understanding of others, including his captors), that person shows that his or her dark night was the gateway to a new and brighter day.

The Escape

By late August 1578, John had survived eight arduous months in his cramped prison. Although he had grown physically weaker, he was determined to escape. He devised a plan and patiently waited for the right moment. He knew he would have to escape by night, making the attempt even more dangerous. When the time seemed right, one day during his recreation, John loosened the bolts on the padlock of his cell door in order to open it later. After dark, leaving his cell, he tied his two bedsheets together. He fastened one end to a convenient hook and placed the other end out a window. Defying danger, he slid down the sheets onto the ledge of the monastery wall. Then he walked along it and jumped down into the street below.

John walked down the street cautiously, for he rightly suspected that the friars would be searching for him. He imposed upon an obliging stranger to let him into his home. In the morning, John set out for his best chance of refuge: Toledo's monastery of Discalced nuns. When he arrived there, the sisters attended to his immediate needs. John was emaciated, sporting a long beard and tattered clothes. His gait was unsteady and his voice weak. The infirmarian served him some cinnamon-flavored pears. The afternoon after he arrived, John went into the monastery's church and began to read aloud the spiritually rich verses he had composed during his confinement. The sisters, assembled for prayer behind their grill, overheard John. Enthralled, the community gathered around John to hear his story and listen to his poetry. They were astounded that he could have produced such sublime religious verses in the midst of his abominable surroundings.

Not surprisingly, the observant Carmelites went looking for John, and before long, they knocked on the nuns' door. The prioress had arranged for him to go into their cloister, a restricted area just for the nuns. When interrogated by the friars, a sister deftly avoided telling all she knew. Her ambiguous response was effective: "It would be a miracle if you were to see any friar here."[5] Those wise women knew they must quickly find a new location for their fugitive. The prioress made contact with one of their friends, Don Pedro Gonzalez, who owned a nearby hospital. He was willing to escort John there by carriage. It was a trip that afforded John time for truly restorative care.

Chapter Six

Moving South to Serve

After convalescing for a month and a half, the still-weak John heard about a gathering of some leaders of the Discalced friars, and he wanted to join them. In October 1578 the meeting was held in Almodóvar de Campo, 180 miles south in the Andalusia region. Don Pedro arranged for John's travel, which included nursing attendants who would remain there with him. Surprised to see him, his Discalced brothers warmly welcomed John.

This was an important meeting for the future of the Reform. The group decided to send delegates to Carmel's worldwide leaders in Italy. They were to explain their perspective on the internal tensions afflicting the Spanish Carmelites, and their ultimate aim was to establish the Discalced of Spain as a separate, self-governing province. John was appointed the temporary prior of a Discalced community at El Calvario in Andalusia, since its prior was among the delegates chosen to go to Rome. Little did John, a true Castilian, realize that he would spend the next decade living in and traveling through that beautiful but unfamiliar and forbidding Andalusian region in southern Spain.

Prior at El Calvario

John obediently accepted his appointment to lead the secluded El Calvario monastery, a two-year-old foundation located near Beas, a town nestled in the splendid hill country. Still tired and weak from his hellish experience in Toledo, John left for El Calvario in the autumn of 1578, accompanied by the attendants Don Pedro had provided. On the way, they stopped for a short stay at the Discalced men's house in La Peñuela, a quiet and austere monastery. John found the environment conducive to prayer and rest. Then they traveled another fifty-five miles and spent a few days at the Discalced nuns' house in Beas. The sisters quickly gauged his high level of faith and wisdom, but also his need for human companionship and care. After he told them of his recent struggles, they sang songs to him about a kind of suffering that leads to love. They quickly grew to esteem John during his short stay. In their company, John started to become his old self again. The nuns and atmosphere at Beas captured John's spirit, and would continue to do so.

Finally, in November, John's little entourage trudged a few more miles over hills and down valleys to reach El Calvario. The needs of the Discalced community there proved a good match for John's gifts. The previous superior had maintained a small, no-frills farmhouse for thirty friars. Some of the men had come to Carmel after spending years as solitaries elsewhere. They ate a sparse diet and their daily schedule included ample time for solitude and prayer. Their simplicity and the detachment from luxury pleased John, who was no slacker in being penitential. Nevertheless, John introduced more balance into the community and enticed the men away from excessive fasting. He enjoyed the company of the friars and treasured the natural splendor of the surroundings. He wanted the whole community to enter into prayer largely by taking greater advantage of the rural beauty, the bright light, and the fresh air. He gradually prodded his confreres toward a prayer marked by discernment of God's providence and by fewer words. Drawing on what he had learned from Teresa, he led the community to grow in both understanding and living the theological virtues of faith, hope, and love. His spiritual conferences on those themes combined well with his efforts to blend prayer with manual labor and community-building activities.

To achieve personal equilibrium, while at El Calvario John began a practice he would continue after his temporary assignment ended. He visited the nearby community of nuns in Beas, walking there each Saturday and returning home on Monday. While at the convent, he heard confessions and offered spiritual guidance to individual sisters. He celebrated Sunday Mass for the nuns, and then he tended their garden. John's own peaceful harmony increased, and the sisters thrived. In the speakroom, John sometimes shared his poetry with them. As he had done for Friar Pedro on the trip to Pastrana and for the nuns at Ávila, after meetings with individual sisters, he handed each one a piece of paper with a nugget of spiritual wisdom.

The effective service John rendered the sisters, however, almost didn't happen. At first the prioress at Beas, Sister Ana of Jesus, was unimpressed when John spoke of Teresa as his "spiritual daughter." When Sister Ana wrote to Teresa to lament this, Teresa let her friend know that she and the nuns at Beas had a gem in their midst. Teresa wrote:

> I was amused, daughter, at how groundless is your complaining, for you have in your very midst *mi padre,* Fray John of the Cross, a heavenly and divine man. I tell you, daughter, from the time he left and went down there I have not found anyone in all Castile like him, or anyone who communicates so much fervor for walking along the way to heaven. You will not believe the feeling of loneliness that his absence causes me. Realize what a great treasure you have there in that saint. All the nuns in your house should speak and communicate with him on matters concerning their soul, and they will see how beneficial it is. They will find themselves making much progress in all that pertains to spirituality and perfection, for our Lord has given him a special grace in this regard. . . . He is a very spiritual man with much experience and learning.[1]

What a difference Teresa's endorsement made. It brought John a warm welcome and open hearts during a peaceful and refreshing segment of his life.

During his stay at El Calvario, or slightly later, John composed the poem *One Dark Night*, titled after his prison escape by night. He also added to his favorite composition, *The Spiritual Canticle*, the poem begun during his harsh confinement. The sisters told him how much they liked his many poems, but they also asked that he explain them. John complied with their request. Over the next decade, he wrote serious theological commentaries on his poems. These writings painstakingly reveal the theology behind the images conveyed in his poems. While John never intended to be an author, his literary brilliance was well worth sharing for the sake of the seekers of spiritual growth. Usually what John wrote touched on matters stemming from his spiritual direction of others.

John's stay at El Calvario lasted from November 1578 to June 1579. He then faced another challenge in Andalusia. He would serve as prior in the new house of studies for the Discalced Carmelite men in the prosperous university city of Baeza, some forty miles away.

On to Busy Baeza

In the summer's heat, John and three of his fellow Discalced friars made their way to Baeza to establish the new foundation. While traveling, John may well have remembered his trip to remote Duruelo years earlier to begin the first Reform foundation of Discalced men. Now, despite John's trials, the work of the Reform was flourishing.

Baeza was a lively municipality of 50,000 inhabitants, and John had much to offer it. He arranged theological discussions featuring presentations on intellectual and spiritual matters, as well as public discussions of case studies in morality. He made himself available to professors and students alike, often meeting them one-on-one. They were quickly and profoundly impressed with his knowledge and wisdom. Many people approached him to talk, and both they and John enjoyed these stimulating conversations. Soon the new foundation opened its rooms to sincere young men who might benefit from exposure to Carmelite life, and some of them discerned a call to that vocation.

In 1580, an influenza epidemic swept through Spain, including John's community in Baeza. As a former hospital attendant, John sprang into action to assist stricken friars. He also visited the sick in hospitals. He again showed himself to be a practical and compassionate man. Amid the challenges, John received sad news. His mother, Catalina, who still lived in Medina del Campo with her older son, Francisco, and his wife, had succumbed to the plague. John must have felt a deep sorrow over this loss. He remembered how his self-sacrificing mother had responded valiantly to the call to love. Long after John had entered Carmel, his mother continued to struggle to make ends meet. The nuns of the Carmelite Reform in Medina del Campo generously supplied her with basic necessities. Quite a few of John's fellow Carmelites knew of his family's low social status and looked down on him, but John never let that hold him back.[2] In fact, he heartily embraced the poverty of both his background and his austere circumstances in Carmel.

As if John didn't have enough to do, during that difficult year of 1580 he was put in charge of another house: Santa Ana, located in a more remote area twenty miles away from Baeza. He began to spread his time and energies between these two places. With more to do for the residents and clients of his two houses, he had less time to help the nuns in Beas, though he still enthusiastically visited them when he could. He was also asked to raise funds for the Discalced way of life, so he sought help from existing and potential donors. His many contacts and projects should dispel any idea that John lived just a quiet life of recollection in these years. To keep himself well rounded, he spent ample time in solitude away from the monastery of Baeza, often at Santa Ana. For days on end, John met God in quiet prayer, to his own benefit and that of the recipients of his prayer-based wisdom. This time away was a necessary counterpoint to the busyness, which tended to wear John down. Thus he lived out a saying he had developed for his directees: "What we need most in order to make progress is to be silent before this great God with our appetites and with our tongue, for the language he best hears is silent love."[3]

Baeza was surely one of the places where Christian spiritual development was in the forefront. Although it was a university community, its learning leaned toward the practical. Here theological studies took a pastoral bent rather than being purely speculative, and they were also oriented toward conversion. This provided a good environment for the ministerially and prayerfully disposed Carmelites of the Reform. The city was also home to many *beatas*, women who worked at secular jobs but lived chastely in their own homes or in small communities.[4] At their best, the *beatas* practiced a life of recollection and aimed at resisting temptations toward evil. At their worst, they were untidy and held distorted views of God and Christian living. Mostly uneducated, some of the *beatas* became overly focused on doing battle with demons and on showy austerities. John was sometimes called upon to serve as an exorcist for them. He did so dutifully and with a longing to form solid disciples of Christ. As a spiritual guide, John wanted to affirm a positive trait he had observed in many of the *beatas*: an inclination toward quiet prayer, a kind of recollection that helped its practitioners to cultivate an abiding intimacy with God.

But a problem clouded the religious climate of Baeza and its *beatas*: the specter of the *Alumbrados* or *Illuminati*, adherents of Illuminism.[5] In Baeza as elsewhere, the *Alumbrados'* rejection of the value of vocal prayer made them suspect. Their penchant for contemplative prayer, however, caused some people to grow wrongly suspicious of inspired teachers of quiet prayer such as John, and Teresa too. When under the scrutiny of the Inquisition as a woman not formally educated in theology, Teresa also had to avoid being classed with these extremists. Although investigated a few times, Teresa had escaped condemnation. It is quite probable that some of his own brother Carmelites referred John to the Inquisition. With his excellent academic credentials, however, John was less subject to such suspicion and more easily dodged the threat of the Inquisition's censure.

John used his many talents at Baeza, and he visited other Discalced communities to help launch or support them. Happiest when at home, John could be at once a practical organizer of the Carmelite house and a wisdom-figure among its members. Not only was he an expert at offering sublime spiritual insights, but he also knew how to arrange for the artistic decoration of the chapels and grounds and was physically able to engage in taxing manual labor.

While leading the house at Baeza, an important development would deeply affect John for the rest of his life. In 1580, Pope Gregory XIII acquiesced to the long-held desire of the Discalced men and women to become a separate province in the

Carmelite order. This meant that the sharp differences between the Reformed and unreformed Carmelites would no longer be played out in everyday encounters on many levels. Now the Discalced could reside in their own communities, with their own superiors to lead them, with their own laws to live by. This ended much of the public conflicts between the two groups. Unfortunately, internal troubles began percolating in the Reform, which would soon afflict John, a man destined to be chosen often for demanding leadership positions.

The members of the Reform held their hope-filled "chapter of separation," their first general meeting, in 1581 at Alcalá de Henares. They needed to choose leaders to guide the new province at a tender juncture. In 1579 Teresa had stated her conviction that the leaders of the Reform should always live and serve in harmony with one another.[6] By a very close vote, perhaps an indication of the underlying discord, Jerome Gracián, Teresa's favorite, was elected provincial over Antonio de Jesus, John's co-pioneer at Duruelo.

A formerly wealthy Italian financier-turned-Carmelite, Nicolas Doria, was chosen as Gracián's first assistant. Teresa, Gracián, and many others had high hopes for Doria's leadership ability. The chapter elected three "definitors," major helpers in governing the province. They included Antonio de Jesus and the ever-useful John of the Cross, who was to remain prior in Baeza for a short time.

John's elevation to office was not surprising. His fellow friars had come to esteem him for his wisdom and his willingness to travel in order to share it with friars, nuns, and lay people. And as a definitor, John's counsel and administrative expertise proved to be widely and frequently sought. This meant that he frequently had to traverse rugged terrain, most often to help the Discalced undertake new foundations. At that time, travel was no leisurely pursuit. Whether by donkey or coach, the going was rough, and the inns along the way were often dirty, poorly managed, and filled with shady characters.

Through it all, John longed to return to Castile, the home of his younger years, which always held a special place in his heart. In a candid self-revelation, John said he felt "abandoned and alone"[7] at Baeza. Although Teresa tried to intervene with Gracián, the provincial, to move John to his native region, Gracián never did. Through John's obedience and humble service, he had come to know firsthand that "the endurance of darkness leads to great light."[8] During his process for beatification years later, those who knew John at this time attested to his seeming contentment and his simple, tranquil ways of engaging people and projects.

John's final meeting with Teresa occurred in late 1581, and it did not proceed as well as he had hoped. He went to Ávila to try to persuade Teresa to go to Granada to help in planning a foundation for the nuns. She demurred and instead sent John to do the job. In Granada, John could not obtain the desired building, and this led to his having to stay in order to deal with complications. He boarded there with the Discalced friars. Little did he know that he was being given a glimpse of his future home.

Chapter Seven

Challenges at Granada

The city of Granada was about ninety miles farther south in Andalusia than Baeza. In June 1581, the friars of the Los Martires (The Martyrs) monastery voted to petition for John as their new prior. Accepting this office demanded a large dose of John's generous spirit, for he would have to move farther away from his beloved Castile. It was a long trip, but when he finally reached Granada, he got a boost from its more tranquil setting. Los Martires was located in an out-of-the-way place, apart from hectic city life. Nearly a decade earlier, a rich civic leader had offered the Discalced friars part of his property for their foundation, but when John arrived, it still needed considerably more construction.

Despite the pleasant natural setting of the monastery, times were tough in both the city and the house. The 1580s were a very interesting but stressful period for the area. Its culture and appearance were being re-Christianized. This southernmost part of Spain had been the bulwark of the Muslim presence, but that population had been in decline following the Christian monarchs' conquest in 1492. To compound the social upheaval, a rash of natural disasters occurred: famine, plague, earthquakes, and floods.

An epidemic struck the area in 1582. John and his brother Carmelites provided food for the needy, much of it collected from the city's more affluent citizens. Los Martires was abuzz with people coming to receive help, but also to give it. The new prior made sure that the poor received not just material goods but also spiritual guidance and the opportunity for confession. The intense activity, however, was a burden on the Discalced community, one that John tried hard to keep at bay. The locals often resisted John's efforts to promote quiet. In the nine years before John's arrival, the established pattern had been that the friars often entertained benefactors, whose assistance the friars had very much needed.

The year 1582 proved an even tougher one for the Discalced because of the death of Teresa of Ávila in October. For years she had suffered from debilitating illnesses. Through it all, and with continued gusto to the end, Teresa had never given up on her quest to found more houses of the Reform. Although John had not seen much of Teresa in the half-decade prior to her death, their deep bond of mutual affection had stayed strong despite their last difficult meeting.

Amid the many challenges he faced at Granada, John also received many graces. The surrounding majestic view of hills and valleys nurtured his aesthetic sensibilities. He also tilled a small garden beside the house, allowing him to be close to God's earth. He had the consolation of seeing many young men find their way to join the community. The 1580s were a decade of great growth for all the Discalced in the Iberian Peninsula. Among Jewish and Muslim converts to Catholicism, the Reform movement's predilection for contemplation was quite appealing. John welcomed about a dozen newcomers each year. His leadership was enhanced when he devised a program of delightful nature-inspired prayer moments and fostered a joyful and fraternal way of life. John would often take a few members of the community out into the hills for walks and prayer. They became better friends of God and of one another for their adventures with their prior. As an adherent of Teresa's vision, John ran the house in a way that emphasized fairness and equality among the brothers, no matter their family backgrounds. He also liked to make the friars laugh. Even when he spoke to them about sublime themes, he would be sure to intersperse amusing tales.

> When he saw one of his subjects sad he would take him by the hand and carry him off for a walk with him in the *huerta* or out in the country and would not leave him until he was cheerful and optimistic again. . . . At recreation he busied himself making little baskets of osier or carving small images in wood with a lancet.[1]

In Granada John undertook construction tasks aplenty. The friars' residence required expansion due to the increasing number of members. Amazingly, John designed and built an aqueduct in order that water might flow into the house from the famous Alhambra palace, located higher on the same hill as Los Martires. This project was no mere hobby. His ever-growing community, as well as the poor people of the town, needed adequate, healthy nourishment. John threw his energies into this venture, which indirectly involved King Philip II. The king realized that if John could find a way to carry water from the Alhambra to the monastery, all of Granada could greatly benefit. By approving the project, the king specifically affirmed his confidence in the Discalced. John also tastefully decorated the building and the grounds, as was his custom, so that they visually bespoke God's beauty and presence.

In seeking help with the construction, John thought of his brother, Francisco, who continued to struggle financially. Like John, he was still mourning their mother's death. When John invited him to assist with the manual labor at Granada, Francisco gladly accepted. What a gift for both of them! John's friars admired Francisco. Like John, he modeled the kind and industrious qualities instilled by their beloved mother, Catalina.

His mother had also taught John how to form good relationships. All through his life, John displayed a capacity for friendly, caring, chaste relationships with consecrated and lay women. While in Granada, two women became his close friends. One was Sister Ana of Jesus, who, ironically, had once made the complaint to Teresa about him. After that awkward start, John had helped her and her sisters in many ways, including the celebration of Mass, confession, and spiritual direction. Hearing the sisters' confessions refined John's appreciation for their way of life and heightened his grasp of the dynamics of the human spirit.

His other cherished friend was Doña Ana del Mercado y Peñuela, with whose family he also established a close bond.

When he had written an intriguing poem, *The Living Flame of Love*, Doña Ana had wanted to understand it better, and she asked him to explain it in a commentary. As was his method, John used the poem as a starting point and went on to develop sublime principles of life lived for God. It took him only fifteen days to produce a theologically profound work based on the highly symbolic poem.

The rural environment of Granada must have inspired John to weave words, but so too did his duty to give frequent formational talks, called conferences, to the community members. The topics of John's conferences fell into three categories. First and foremost, he spoke frequently of the contemplative recollection needed by friars. John wanted people to know themselves as God's most beloved creatures, and reflect on their lives in a world filled with vestiges of God the Creator. Second, John reminded the men of their privilege to be apostolic friars, sent to announce the Gospel. They were like the apostles in the New Testament and so many others over the centuries. He realized they could greatly assist in God's work of guiding people toward living holy lives worthy of heaven. Third, John addressed the way of growth in holiness by means of the virtues. This not only included the theological virtues of faith, hope, and love, but also the associated human, moral virtues, which spell out what it means to love. Even more, John would sometimes invite his household to "decorate our brothers," by which he meant that each friar should suggest virtues for another friar to strive to develop.[2] He would urge them all to pray for each other.

Continual Conflicts

Unfortunately, the leadership of the Discalced Carmelites' first provincial, Gracián, proved problematic. A division grew between those who favored a strict following of the Discalced province's laws of fast and abstinence, as well as the rule of remaining in one's cell in quiet prayer, and those who advocated a greater active ministry, which required more travel. Gracián was in the latter group. He journeyed much, and he promoted sending Discalced men from Spain to missionary lands. Three times he assigned men to Africa. Sadly, the first two expeditions failed. The first group drowned due to shipwreck, and the second group was attacked by pirates and had to return. The third group did arrive, but the controversial action remained a source of anguish and internal dispute for the Reform. Gracián was still firmly committed to missionary endeavors, but others, including Gracián's first assistant, Father Doria, cautioned against pursuing this ideal at that delicate time. Gracián, however, wanted to send missionaries to Mexico. John saw promise in this effort, but feared an overemphasis on action would override Carmel's need for contemplative prayer. Still, in John's role as a definitor, he supported the initiative. Discalced Carmelite missionaries began going from Spain to Mexico in 1585.

Another conflict arose because some of the friars thought Gracián spent too much time with the Discalced nuns—a criticism also leveled against John and other friars. Tensions festered. Among the Discalced, a move to censure Gracián succeeded. This forceful act, which took place at an interim provincial chapter, was largely arranged by Doria. He had become the official liaison between the province and the Carmelite Prior General. Doria found Gracián's way of leading much too mild, and he took a strong stance on the matter of the relations between friars and nuns. Doria saw the ordained friars as called to help the nuns, but not by befriending and conversing with them. He favored a model of governance that stressed the nuns' dependence on the authority of the priests. Doria could be harsh in his way of dealing with others. For that reason, even the members who were dissatisfied with Gracián's leadership did not favor Doria. John, like Gracián, had been a favorite counselor and spiritual friend to so many Discalced women. These various disputes troubled John and strained relations among the members when they so keenly needed peace as the new province took shape. In most respects, John stood for a stricter interpretation of the Carmelite way of life than did Gracián, but John the definitor remained objective, open, and notably respectful of the first Discalced provincial.

In these turbulent 1580s, John gave himself wholeheartedly to the day-to-day work of building up the Discalced, spiritually and practically. He spearheaded the start of five new monasteries for men and three for women. For many of these sites, property had to be purchased and buildings built or renovated. John was deeply involved in the transactions for the new foundations, and his economic and social prowess showed itself repeatedly. For example, he knew how to find bargains, but more crucially, his shrewd grasp of human nature helped him to select the right combination of members to form the fledgling communities.

While opening a new house was a joyful event, and holding office an honor, John found these services burdensome. The meetings of the provincial leaders led to some beneficial plans, but inevitably also to frequent disagreements about the Carmelite values and practices to uphold and foster. John took seriously his role of discerning what was needed for the good of all. More and more he found some Reform leaders promoted their own ideas too passionately. One difficult issue concerned the role of benefactors, especially the type John had encountered in Granada. John's experiences convinced him that courting the presence of benefactors and their demands could threaten the balance of the community's fraternal life, simplicity, solitude, and service. In 1583, John was strongly criticized at a chapter meeting for his stance. Less than two years later, as he helped to establish a new community of nuns at Malaga, he wrote: "It was founded in poverty without any temporal backing. May God be pleased to preserve it."[3]

In 1586, an event occurred that symbolizes his calm approach to life and leadership. While in Cordoba at a newly opened foundation still under construction, a large wall collapsed into John's room. His fellow friars came running and, in the clearing dust, found John safe in a corner. The friars expected him to be distraught, but John laughed off the incident and gave credit for his safety to Mary—his childhood protector. Some time later, when that same community installed a statue of Mary given to them by a benefactor, John ordered that it be returned. He thought it better depicted a woman of luxury rather than the simple Mary, Our Lady of Mount Carmel, whom he knew and loved.

During much of his stay in Granada, John served as both the prior and a prominent provincial leader, heavily involved in the general governance of the friars and nuns of the Reform.

From 1585 to 1587, John served as vicar provincial, chief assistant to the strong-willed new provincial, Doria. Under Doria's leadership, conflict escalated due to his harsh way of dealing with people. Doria introduced a centralized, exacting approach to Carmelite life that caused many Discalced vociferously to criticize him for leading the province away from the spirit of Teresa. Among Doria's critics were the ex-provincial Gracián and the nuns whom Gracián urged to write letters for use at a chapter meeting. John certainly concurred with many of Gracián's fears, but he also saw some benefits in Doria's governing style. John refrained from joining in any sharp words against Doria at that time.

A hallmark of John's approach to Carmelite life was that he prized its combination of three elements: the eremitical (hermit-like), cenobitical (community-centered), and mendicant (open to going out to serve as needed) lifestyles. While John respected all three elements, the Discalced friars chronically disagreed over how to blend them in a single way of life. In his travels as first assistant to the provincial, John often had to settle conflicts over these matters in everyday community life. He showed wisdom and courage during an incident at the Los Remedios monastery in Seville, where two traveling preachers, Diego Evangelista and Francisco Crisostomo, were spending too much time outside the monastery. John decided to take a stand to prohibit them from this practice. While their ministry of the word was worthwhile, John concluded, their excessive absence from community was not in keeping with the Reform. When John confronted them, neither man accepted his correction graciously, and they both harbored strong resentment toward John.

John also vigorously addressed a pressing question: Should outgoing superiors be eligible for immediate reelection? From his own experience, John thought that, at the end of their terms, superiors should have some relief from the burden of authority. Not only would it benefit the superior's growth in humility, but the community would also profit from the fresh insights of a different leader. John vulnerably held to his minority stance, which a chapter meeting did not endorse. Although the chapter members respected John's position for its high ideals, they reasonably decided that the community did not have enough men qualified to be superiors. Ideals had to yield to realities.

Continual conflict existed between Doria, "an ascetic, hard-nosed bureaucrat," and his predecessor, Gracián, often viewed as "a charming but naive man of affairs."[4] While John had often defended Gracián, for his part Gracián never defended or praised John. And Doria used John's gifts as much as he could benefit from them, but often in an opportunistic way.[5] John increasingly took courageous positions that varied from the ideas of different factions.

During this challenging period, a humorous incident occurred that reveals John's practical wisdom and kindness. While staying at a monastery in Manchuela, John, who had been quite sick, was told to eat meat. The friar who served as the cook wanted to please John, and so he prepared a succulent partridge for his meal. When the cook carelessly left the dish unattended, a cat ate half of the bird. Ashamed, the friar apologized profusely to John, who laughed as he told the friar not to worry. He offered his fellow friar consolation rather than censure, telling him not to fret over something so small.

In 1587, John continued as a definitor but no longer as vicar provincial. Since he still resided at Granada, he resumed the position of prior. Over the years, his familiar presence and the improvements he made to the monastery made a big difference. Granada's Discalced house was acclaimed as the best in Spain, along with its lush garden, which was attributable to John's aqueduct. More importantly, John's spiritual leadership and his writings were becoming renowned.

However, John would soon see fulfilled his long-desired return to Castile as the Carmelites of the Reform drew increasingly on his energies.

Chapter Eight

Waning Light and Growing Darkness

In 1588, John moved to Segovia in the region of Castile, where he finally lived closer to his roots, because Rome had declared the province of the Discalced friars and nuns to be a congregation. As such, it would be established with a powerful vicar general taking the helm for a six-year term, assisted by six friars serving as his council, called the "Consulta." Father Doria had tested a version of this governing model in his first few years as provincial and, with Rome's backing, he was now ready to make it definitive. The model centralized authority in the chief leaders and lessened the collegiality of the local priors. Notably, the arrangement granted the vicar general great authority to discipline or expel the members he judged strongly divisive. Gracián remained a vocal opponent of Doria's arrangement, but soon its procedures would significantly affect him and John.

The new congregation convoked its first general chapter in 1588 at Madrid. Doria was elected to the new top office, but hardly by a landslide. Many friars were supporters of Gracián, who had refused to attend. Doria planned to relegate Gracián as the superior in faraway Mexico, but when that plan didn't work out, the humiliated Gracián was reduced to being a simple friar. Gracián obeyed, but he continued to place allegiance to his sense of what Teresa would have wanted above his compliance with Doria's policies.

In this highly charged political situation, John was elected the third definitor, making him a coordinator of the Consulta. He also became a close associate of Doria's, who thought John an ally in opposing much of Gracián's more lenient approach to Discalced life. This spelled tension, for while John knew Gracián was flawed, he still respected his fellow friar. John could sense trouble brewing as the congregation's new slate of leaders went into action. Being perceptive, he probably expected to get caught in the middle.

The Discalced priory at Segovia, with its novitiate and philosophical college, was chosen for the congregation's headquarters. Therefore the house needed an esteemed, versatile prior, and John fit the bill. He would again be wearing a few different hats. The priory required extensive reconstruction and expansion, and John had proved himself capable of supervising such a project. He put to work a varied group of laborers: a few hired hands who lived at the site, some helpful neighbors, and sometimes the entire community of friars.

When a friend told John how much he was intrigued at John's enjoyment at working with rocks and building materials, John humorously but tellingly replied: "Don't be surprised, son, for when I am dealing with them I have fewer sins to confess than when I am dealing with men."[1] John humbly looked at his own weaknesses, as he expressed in a treasured maxim about the darkness that creeps into human encounters: "Lord, you return gladly and lovingly to lift up the one who offends you, but I do not turn to raise and honor the one who annoys me."[2] John knew that the fruit of God's compassion toward us shows in our compassion toward others.

During his years in Segovia John offset his struggles with his preferred pastimes: taking up construction tools and supervising the workers; offering expert spiritual direction to friars, nuns, and lay people, including some influential leaders; spending time with good friends. Doña Ana de Peñalosa esteemed John so greatly that she moved from Andalusia to Segovia to be near him. John enjoyed the company of Father Villegas, a priest whose erudition and companionship enriched John's spirit. He also welcomed visits from his brother, Francisco. Most of all, he devoted himself to long periods of solitude and deep intimacy with God. John did not compose new works in Segovia, but he kept in mind the rich ideas he had penned, which helped to sustain him during this stormy period.

Recurring Challenges

A continuing issue for the congregation and for John concerned the governance of the Discalced nuns. Doria strongly pushed for giving their oversight of them to the whole Consulta. John and others, including most of the nuns, favored appointing one friar as the nuns' superior. That friar would then develop a focused connection with them and their needs. Sister Ana of Jesus was worriedly intent on staving off Doria's approach. She angered him by organizing some nuns to write directly to the Pope about the matter, instead of appealing through Doria. This became quite a tangled issue for everyone, especially John. Although a good friend to Sister Ana of Jesus, John disagreed with her direct appeal to Rome. Still, he spoke forthrightly in the Consulta in favor of the nuns' opinion.

John's insights were firmly rooted in his own prayerful reflection. Serving closely with Doria, John disagreed more and more with his forceful superior about his ideas and leadership style. John found himself becoming Doria's opponent. Compounding the situation was the reality that many of the Reform's newer recruits lacked a contemplative disposition—they either strongly courted Doria's favor or lacked the courage or insight to offer thoughts that challenged their leader's ideas.

In the midst of the conflict over governing the Discalced nuns, Sister Ana of Jesus told John that if the nuns were to have one designated superior, she hoped it would be him. John told her he expected a very different outcome. And he was right. Ultimately, the Pope backed Doria.

In June 1591, the Carmelites of the Reform convoked their next chapter in Madrid. John and Doria held opposite views on most of the main themes discussed. John respectfully criticized the excessive number of laws Doria had set in place, as well as their harshness. Having known Teresa in the early days of the

Reform, John found Doria's vision not in keeping with that of La Madre. He also lamented Doria's poor treatment of Gracián. Moreover, given the tense atmosphere prevailing in the congregation and at the chapter, John strongly pleaded for voting by secret ballot. John was virtually alone in all of these stances—certainly an unenviable position, but one John's conscience and prayer demanded of him. His forthright disagreement enraged Doria, who had come to realize that the gentle friar was not the puppet that he had wanted.

Although more than seventy friars had emerged as leaders by the end of the chapter, John was not among them. When a friend offered his sympathy over the rejection, John's reply expressed what he most valued and showed his great confidence in a provident God:

> Do not let what is happening to me, daughter, cause you any grief, for it does not cause me any. What greatly grieves me is that the one who is not at fault is blamed. Men do not do these things, but God, who knows what is suitable for us and arranges things for our good. Think nothing else but that God ordains all, and where there is no love, put love, and you will draw out love.[3]

John had been deposed from leadership, and though bitterness might tug at him, it would not overtake him. He would make love his supreme response.

John's future was now uncertain. While the state of the Reform saddened him, John knew God would keep leading the Discalced in the right direction. It was not John's place to question what God was bringing about; he felt at peace that he had spoken up for what he thought was right.

Ironically, Doria's first plan was to send John to Mexico to take the role he had once planned for Gracián. John agreed to this move, and some of his confreres wrongly surmised he had been forced into this. However, since the Pope had settled the matter of the nuns' governance, it became less crucial for Doria to get John out of the way. Indeed, wanting to capitalize on John's talents and the respect many of the Discalced had for him, Doria decided that John should go back to Segovia as prior. John pleaded with Doria not to assign him there, knowing well that it would continue to be a hotbed of tension. Relenting in the end, Doria reverted to his idea of sending John to Mexico, but first assigned him to La Peñuela for a short time. As a young friar, John had stopped at La Peñuela for some rest. Now, in its quiet surroundings, John would have to select twelve men of the Reform and prepare them for assignment to Mexico, where John would be their prior.

How did John manage to carry on despite all his sufferings? On one of Francisco's visits to Segovia, John confided his secret. He told his brother that once, while praying in front of an image of Christ carrying his Cross, he had heard Christ speaking to him: "Friar John, ask what favor you will of me, and I will grant it in return for the services you have done me." John replied: "Lord, make me to suffer and be despised for your sake."[4] Francisco probably found it hard to understand these stark words, but they expressed John's trust in Christ, whose faithfulness to his Father's will led to suffering and death—but ultimately to resurrection. While John did not mean that suffering and being despised were good in themselves, he knew that they were the inevitable side effects of doing what was right. Thus they would lead him down Christ's own path. John had come to know that to suffer for Gospel values could be a gateway to growth in knowing, loving, and serving God. This insight signifies John's advanced spiritual state and is the idea underlying one of his famous but misunderstood maxims: "Endeavor to be inclined always: not to the easiest, but to the most difficult; not to the most delightful, but to the most distasteful."[5]

La Peñuela and Úbeda

John hoped to stay at La Peñuela until his departure for the Mexican expedition. He was happy to be there for a period of prayer and reflection, which he needed after suffering humiliation at the Madrid chapter. In a letter of August 19, 1591 to Doña Ana de Peñalosa, he wrote honestly:

> I like it very much, glory to God, and I am well. The vastness of the desert is a great help to the soul and body, although the soul fares very poorly. The Lord must be desiring that it have its spiritual desert. Well and good if it be for his service. . . . This morning we have already returned from gathering our chickpeas, and so the mornings go by. On another day we shall thresh them. It is nice to handle these mute creatures, better than being badly handled by living ones. God grant that I may stay here. . . . Take care of your soul. . . . Look after your health, and do not fail to pray when you can.[6]

John also enjoyed serving as spiritual director to his fellow friars. Never one to miss an opportunity to assist as needed, he managed to compose a book, which has long since been lost, about the difference between authentic and false miracles. It was probably at La Peñuela that he produced the revised editions of his commentaries *The Spiritual Canticle* and *The Living Flame of Love*. He supported all his confreres. One day, a friar accidentally started a small fire in the house. John's decisive directives, prayers, and compassion for that friar and others left their positive mark on the community long after the event.

As often happened for John, things did not go as planned. Less than two months after arriving in La Peñuela, John came down with a fever. He also suffered from gangrene, with ulcerous sores. A serious infection in his right leg spread throughout his body, but medical attention did not improve his condition. He expressed with resignation that he could no longer envision himself among those preparing to leave for Mexico. Undaunted, he lived according to words he had written: "Love works so in me that whether things go well or badly love turns them to one sweetness."[7] A man of much experience, John knew well that not everything that happens will *feel* sweet, but he trusted in God's provident love to bring about what is ultimately right and good.

John obeyed the orders of his superior at La Peñuela, who sent him to a different house for cure and more rest. Given the choice between two locations, John chose Úbeda over Baeza, because he knew he would be less well known there and so less prone to receiving the adulation of visiting well-wishers. He set out for Úbeda in late September.

Before John's departure, Friar Diego Evangelista, now a congregational definitor and visitor general, made more trouble for his ailing former superior. As vicar provincial of Andalusia John had once chided Evangelista for being too much of a gadabout. Now, as John's physical condition deteriorated, Evangelista spoke of him disparagingly wherever he traveled in the waning months of 1591. Evangelista traveled widely to investigate the propriety of the relationship Gracián and John had with the nuns of the Reform. In Evangelista's investigatory process—which was unchallenged by Doria—he and his collaborators visited convents and priories seeking evidence maligning Gracián. Evangelista wanted John removed from the Carmelite order on the charge he had excessive affection for the nuns of the Reform. Evangelista probed for any evidence that might somehow incriminate John. Fortunately, those attempts did not succeed. Evangelista never did come to view John positively; in fact he tore him down as much after his death as he had during his life. Faced with Evangelista's bullying tactics, many Discalced nuns and friars tried to protect John's reputation. In an effort to avoid providing any fodder for Diego's false claims, they burned John's letters and writings as well as any portraits of him—a tragic loss for the ages.

Úbeda was a grueling day's journey away from La Peñuela, and John arrived there on September 28, 1591. Despite its isolation, it was not the ideal place for John. The prior, Friar Francisco Crisostomo, also bore a grudge against John, his former superior at Los Remedios, for curtailing his preaching trips. He placed John in the worst cell of the monastery, and he complained of the expense of caring for the invalid. Another, more sympathetic friar let the regional superior know of John's harsh treatment. That superior was none other than Friar Antonio de Heredia, John's co-pioneer at Duruelo twenty-three years earlier. Friar Antonio came and stayed with John at Úbeda for an extended time. His visit succeeded in affirming John, insuring his charitable treatment, and nudging if not forcing the prior to change his ways.

While at Úbeda, John learned of Evangelista's investigation. At that moment in his life, facing deadly illness, he could have become overwhelmed with bitterness. When advised to appeal to Doria, John dismissed the idea. Instead, he humbly trusted that the truth would prevail and God would vindicate him. Writing to a fellow friar, John explained: "Son, don't trouble yourself about this, for they cannot take away my habit except for incorrigibility or disobedience and I am entirely ready to amend in anything for which I have erred and to accept any penance they may give me."[8] In conversation with a trusted friar, he further reflected: "I only desire that in the inquiries nothing is done to offend God."[9]

In December, John's condition worsened as more of his body became infected. Unable to move easily, a rope was placed over John's bed for him to lift himself to gain some minimal relief. All the while, John prayed with the friars. Even in Úbeda townspeople and friends still sought him out. While their visits were consoling and prayer-filled, they must have also been tiring for John. In his illness, he steeped himself in biblical words. The Book of Psalms gave him particular support, and his beloved Song of Songs provided the backdrop for his final days.

In the afternoon of Friday, December 12, John, sensing he would die on Saturday, requested to speak with Crisostomo. John sincerely apologized for the trouble his illness and impending death were causing the community. Moved with pity and newfound respect for John, the formerly hostile prior broke into tears. From then on, he held John in great esteem.

Witnesses later told of the contentment John expressed with the prospect of going home to God on a Saturday, which the Church has traditionally celebrated as Mary's day. To the end, this devoted brother of Our Lady of Mount Carmel longed to be associated with Mary, his Savior's mother, his childhood protector, and his order's inspiration. His fellow friars at Úbeda included some longstanding supporters and a few opponents, most of whom John won over by his graciousness and patience. As they gathered around him in prayer, John might well have remembered his own care for the dying at the plague hospital in Medina del Campo decades before. As his brother Carmelites praised him for all the good he had done, his reply was typically God-centered: "This is not the time to be thinking of that; it is by the merits of the blood of our Lord Jesus Christ that I hope to be saved."[10]

When his confreres told him they would soon be praying the breviary prayer of Matins, John responded peacefully that he would be praying it also, but in heaven. He perceived that his end had come, and he asked that verses from the Song of Songs be recited. As midnight approached, he felt death drawing near. Indeed, John left this world very early on the morning of Saturday, December 14, at age forty-nine. The last words from his lips were those of Jesus, his Redeemer, as he hung on the cross: "Into your hands, Lord, I commend my spirit." Since 1970, the Church has celebrated December 14 as John's feast day.

Two years after John's death, the Discalced were elevated to the status of an independent order, largely through the efforts of Doria, about a year before his own death. Gracián had continued to support the nuns in their resistance to Doria's determination to alter their constitutions. Because Gracián kept in close communication with the nuns, his reputation declined more and more, to the extent that the Carmelites expelled him from the order in 1592, just two months after John's death. Four years later, Pope Clement VIII, without restoring him to membership, allowed Gracián to live among the observant Carmelites, but according to the rule of the Discalced. Gracián did so until he died in 1614, having given years of service to the Church.

The life of Juan (John) de Yepes y Álvarez could be seen as a "rags to riches" story, but in an unusual sense. Born materially poor, John nevertheless received a splendid education and combined it with his thriving practice of prayer. He died spiritually rich, having permanently committed himself to live the solemn promise of poverty he had made as a young man. He faced repeated rejection and suspicion, but was never anything but kind, honest, and authentically human. When he succumbed to illness at age forty-nine, after a lifetime of trials endured with equanimity and joyful love, he left behind few personal effects but many achievements. John of the Cross died as he had lived, convinced that the Cross of Christ leads us to love and is fruitful. His wealth, not of material possessions but of wisdom and holiness, had already enriched the lives of countless people and had brought him much deserved acclaim. His writings and reputation brilliantly live on long after his death.

Appendix

A Spiritually Rich Teaching to Share

The sisters at Beas, who once asked John to clarify his ideas, deserve lasting thanks. Their encouragement inspired him to write down his insights. One could summarize John's main points, concerning how a Christian who wants to grow spiritually should progress, as follows (written in first person for clarity):

> I desire to know, love, and serve God, and to live a good, moral life. Yet, I find I lack the power to achieve what I desire. My disordered desires and choices hold me back from making progress. Also, I dislike the suffering entailed in more deeply following Christ. I need an inflow of God's strength to help me make progress spiritually. I ask God to give that to me as I try to pray and live well.
>
> I enjoy a "first fervor" or a "honeymoon" as I begin to progress. With that, I give up old ways of selfishness.

I choose to be faithful to good ways of praying and living. My prayer uses thoughts, words, and imagination. God gives me consolation, which boosts my momentum, and I experience this help in the satisfaction of praying well and living virtuously. As I feel God's love, that feeling helps me to make progress. And so, at my best, I exchange inordinate, badly directed pleasures for the pleasure of God's consolation. My motive, in fact, is still largely to enjoy such consolations. I seem to be in control of my good progress.

Becoming more receptive to God's lead as I make progress, I am open to being less motivated by the satisfaction I get from good praying and living. I start to detach myself from my dependence on God's consolations, and I adjust to God's gentle, guiding presence in my life. Adjusting to this, however, brings me distress. I miss the novelty of the joy and pleasure I felt as I started to progress. I now feel disoriented as I think that I could do better at attaining that sense of satisfaction I formerly felt. But I also am discovering that I do not need consolations and satisfaction to grow spiritually, for God is present to me even when the consolations I used to experience in prayer are gone. I am growing in virtue as I practice doing God's will for higher motives, not primarily for what pleases me or for what I can get out of it. The withdrawal of God's consolation is good because that leads me to steadily love God for the right motives. I need to keep remembering that good prayer and good living do not depend upon good feelings. By withdrawing consolations, God is inviting me into faithful, ever more trusting perseverance in Christian living—into the practice of virtue.

As I move further into a post-honeymoon period, I am called to be more responsive to God's lead. I am becoming more docile, as I want to do what God wants for me. My relationship with God is moving toward being more sober, genuine, and peaceful. To make progress, I need to be receptive to growing in faith, hope, and love, which are gifts of God. My prayer ought to be a more contemplative and simpler prayer, wherein I rest in God's presence. God is inviting me and helping me to see life and people as he sees them and to love as he loves.

Having become more attentive and responsive to God's promptings in my life, I let God lead me into deeper, more intense purification and transformation. This will involve some more detachment and some real suffering. Yet, I keep praying to God and I keep loving others. Occasionally, I profoundly experience God's acts of love for me.

If I make substantial progress, then rationalization and defensiveness have ebbed away. I am habitually united with God in my prayer and in my ever more virtuous life.

Poetic Images Drawn from John's Life Experience

Some of the most memorable images John used in his writings are worth exploring, for they vividly describe the dynamics of our life with God. As a poet, John had a deep awareness of images and their impact. As Crisogono notes, John had "a fantasy which gathers together all the beauties of visible creation in meadows, wooded mountains and river banks, night and early morning. . . ."[1] He drew his favorite images from his everyday world. Immersing himself in the writings of earlier spiritual masters, John undoubtedly discovered how powerfully images speak of the Christian's efforts to follow Christ and seek union with God. Four images stand out prominently in John's writing: night and its darkness, a log tossed into a flame, a romantic relationship leading to marriage, and a mountain climb. These images would become some of the hallmarks of John's own later acclaimed contributions to the Catholic spiritual tradition.

Night

Night is a time that succeeds yesterday and leads into tomorrow. People in the sixteenth century had a sharper sense of the contrast between day and night than we do. Whereas we can extend the benefits of daylight by artificial lighting, John and his contemporaries saw the night for what it naturally is: a time of darkness that can be scary or restful, one that makes travel risky but also promises a fresh new day. As a time for restorative sleep, night reminds us that we cannot always control what happens, just as we cannot control our dreams.

Night is thus a time of transition. Similarly, our relationship with God will call us to make changes so we can grow in holiness and in the depths of prayer. Some changes are inevitable when things happen to us that call for our openness or surrender to them. Other changes are more freely chosen, so we can direct them. In some ways, the night is a time for one to be "passive," as John worded it. We might call this being "receptive" or "open" to

God's providence and to life's realities. We need to be receptive to what God is doing, in ways we do not make happen. We can let God move us to a fuller, holier future as we let God draw us to new ways of thinking and acting. At night, we also decide certain things as we make our way through the darkness. These decisions make our engagement with night somewhat "active," as John called it. We need to do what we can, using God's gifts to us, to decide and act in God-like ways: being virtuous, filled with faith, hope, and love, and being consciously detached from what would lead us to sin and would distract us from deepening our friendship with God. John's poem *One Dark Night* and his commentary *The Dark Night* point to these realities. John covers these topics in much of his writings, and the commentary gives special attention to the more passive aspects of spiritual growth.

Flame of Love

In John's time, heat was not so easily available. While the image of a log tossed into a fire and then consumed by the flame is familiar to us, it was then more crucial. John thought of the human person as having great potential for close communion with God. But our imperfections require that we be purified, just as flames consume a log. John's poem and commentary, both titled *The Living Flame of Love*, explore these ideas in particular.[2] He pictured God as the flame, blazing with love, truth, and the power to heat and enlighten us spiritually. When the log is tossed into the flame, the work of union happens slowly but surely. Still, God always remains distinct from any of us. This image reminds us of how much God can do when we are surrounded by his mysteriously working but consuming presence and allow it to fill us. John taught: "To undertake the journey to God the heart must be burned with the fire of divine love and purified of all creatures [inordinate attachments to ideas, things, people]."[3]

Climbing a Mountain

John knew that one of the most dominant and helpful metaphors for the Christian life is that of a journey. Living in hilly areas, John was drawn to imagine a particular kind of journey: the adventure of climbing a mountain. Important biblical figures typically met God on the summit of a mountain, such as Moses on Mount Sinai. Using the Carmelites' communal memory of its cherished Mount Carmel in the Holy Land, John took the climbing of that mountain as a metaphor for advancing in one's relationship with God. John once drew a rough but detailed sketch of what is entailed in making it to the mountaintop, which signifies near-complete union with God in this life. To reach that high point, he showed that the wayfarer must be attached to the ways of God and detached from whatever could hinder progress. Pilgrims need resources to scale a mountain. What we carry in life, tangible or intangible, should help us to climb. Even if what we carry is something good in itself, our wrong use of it can block spiritual progress. John is the guide who has made it to the top and wants you to get there too. He can coach you to avoid pitfalls. He can urge you to settle for nothing less than the mountaintop, no matter how alluring are the views along the way. Christ supports us as we climb, with the Holy Spirit as our true guide. We encounter our God in a more perfect way at the end of a successful ascent. In *Ascent of Mount Carmel*, John tells us much about what to choose and how to act as we climb the mountain toward greater closeness to God.

Spiritual Marriage

From the Catholic spiritual tradition, John inherited the theme of spiritual marriage as symbolizing the Christian's relationship with God. John probably heard of his parents' love for each other in their short marriage, and he witnessed the faithful, marital commitment of his brother, Francisco, to Ana, despite all the losses they endured. Songs John heard in Spanish streets told of romance, betrothal, and marital love. John transposed these to describe the praying Christian's deepening love for the Savior. The central characters in the Old Testament's Song of Songs, the lover and the beloved, came to life especially in John's *Spiritual Canticle.* There John offered a panorama of the joy, the questioning, the longing, and the pleasure and pain involved in a loving relationship.

. . . .

Prayer in Honor of Saint John of the Cross

Loving God, you gave your son, Saint John of the Cross, the gift of steadfast love for you and the faith to believe that you are always close to us. May we desire to be detached from whatever might keep us from knowing, loving, and serving you as completely as possible. When life is challenging and discouraging for us, as it often was for John, give us a share in John's courage. When a transition looms in life, give us the kind of flexibility John mustered to keep committed to you. If we start to lose our zest for life, for any reason, help us to be like John in finding joy in the gifts that surround us. If conflict threatens, provide us the peace that John maintained in trying situations. We ask this through Jesus Christ, your Son, our Redeemer and Brother, and through the intercession of John of the Cross, our brother.

• • • • • • • • • • • • •

Reflection Questions

1. Have you seen or experienced how various kinds of poverty can lead either toward a growing connection to God or toward vices such as sadness, bitterness, envy, and greed? What attitudes or decisions can turn people toward God rather than toward negative ways of thinking and acting?
2. John helped people to see prayer as an intimate sharing with God, rather than merely reciting words without much thought. How would you describe your way of praying? What personal qualities or gifts do you have that might lead you to a quiet, more contemplative way of praying?
3. John's life was one of detachment from the things that people often value as important for their lives. As a young

man, he was very poor. As a Carmelite, he promised to live a life of poverty. In his later years, he was deprived of some of the satisfactions that might have made his life easier. How do you think John's detachment, voluntary and involuntary, helped him to grow in his relationship with God?

. . . .

Chronology

1542—Juan (John) de Yepes is born at Fontiveros, Spain, to Gonzalo de Yepes and Catalina Álvarez. (The exact date of his birth is disputed, and sometimes put at June 24.)

ca. 1546—John's father, Gonzalo, dies at Fontiveros after a long illness.

ca. 1548—John's brother Luis dies of malnutrition at Fontiveros.

ca. 1548—Catalina and her surviving sons, Francisco and John, relocate to Arevalo.

ca. 1551—Catalina moves with her sons to Medina del Campo.

ca. 1552—John attends the School of Doctrine, a residential trade school conducted by sisters.

ca. 1557—John works as a hospital attendant at Las Bubas, Medina del Campo's plague hospital.

ca. 1559—John takes courses at the Jesuit-run college in Medina del Campo.

1562—Teresa of Ávila founds the first reformed Carmelite convent for women, Saint Joseph's at Ávila.

1563—John enters the Carmelite monastery of Santa Ana in Medina del Campo.

1564–68—John undertakes studies in Salamanca.

1567—John is ordained to the priesthood and soon afterward meets Teresa of Ávila at Medina del Campo.

August 1568—John accompanies Teresa on a trip to Valladolid. On the way she orients him to the values and practices of her Reform. Soon afterward, John becomes one of the pioneers at Duruelo, the first men's house of the Reform.

November 28, 1568—With the visit of the local Carmelite provincial to Duruelo, John and a few confreres take vows to live according to the Carmelite Reform.

June 1570—John and the entire Duruelo community move to Mancera de Abajo, and John briefly stays at Pastrana to assist in the formation of new members.

April 1571—John leaves Mancera to become prior at Alcalá de Henares, the house of studies for Carmelite men of the Reform.

Early 1572—John is sent for a few months to Pastrana to help provide sound formation to Carmelites there. He later returns to Alcalá.

May 1572—At Teresa's request John is assigned as the confessor for nuns of the Incarnation Convent in Ávila, where Teresa has become prioress.

December 1575—John is arrested and brought for a short period to the men's monastery in Medina del Campo, but is soon released.

December 3, 1577—Kidnapped by observant Carmelites, John is blindfolded and taken to the Toledo monastery's jail and held in miserable conditions.

August 1578—One night, John escapes and recuperates in various locations in Toledo.

October 1578—John attends a meeting of leaders of the men's Reform in the Andalusian region. Afterward he is sent as temporary prior to that region's El Calvario monastery.

June 1579—John is assigned as prior in Baeza.

1580—Catalina, John's mother, dies during an epidemic at Medina del Campo.

1581—The Carmelites of the Reform in Spain are designated a separate province, with Jerome Gracián as provincial. John is chosen as a "definitor," a high-level leader. He travels to consult with Teresa. This is their last visit.

1582—Still a definitor, John moves to Granada to be the prior of its Los Martires community.

October 1582—After years of declining health, Teresa of Ávila dies at sixty-seven.

1585—Remaining a resident of Granada but not its prior, John becomes vicar provincial, serving closely with the new provincial, Nicholas Doria.

1587—Still in provincial leadership, John again becomes prior of Granada.

1588—John is raised to the position of leader of the new Consulta, the governing body of the Discalced, amid strong tensions in the Reform. He becomes prior of Segovia in his native region of Castile.

June 1591—Turned out of office, John moves through La Peñuela, where his health breaks down. He moves to Úbeda.

December 14, 1591—John dies just after midnight at Úbeda.

1675—John is beatified.

1726—John is canonized, with November 24 as his feast day.

1926—John is declared a Doctor of the Church.

1970—John's feast day is moved to his date of death, December 14.

1990—Pope John Paul II shares with the world his letter *Master in the Faith*, in honor of the 400th anniversary of John's death.

. . . .

Notes

Introduction

1. Peter Tyler, *St. John of the Cross* (New York: Continuum, 2010), 2.

2. Kieran Kavanaugh, *John of the Cross: Doctor of Light and Love* (New York, Crossroad, 1999), 11.

3. John Paul II, *Master in the Faith*, December 14, 1990, no. 1.

4. Daughters of Saint Paul, *Heavenly Friends: A Saint for Each Day* (Boston: Pauline Books & Media, 1958, 1986).

Chapter One

1. Scholars disagree as to whether Gonzalo had Jewish blood, but many would hold that he did. Indeed, he came from an area (Toledo) that contained a high population of Jews. Catalina's background is also disputed. She hailed from a part of Castile with a high Muslim population, and she practiced an occupation (weaving) commonly

practiced by Arab Muslims. She often lived in areas populated by Moriscos.

2. Some historians would place John's birth a year or two earlier than 1542.

3. Leonard Doohan, *The Dark Night Is Our Only Light* (Self-published, 2013), 4.

4. "St. John of the Cross: A New Image," in *God Speaks in the Night*, trans. and ed. Kieran Kavanaugh and Federico Ruiz (Washington, DC: ICS Publications, 1991), vi.

5. John of the Cross, *The Spiritual Canticle*, commentary, st. 1, par. 8, in *The Collected Works of St. John of the Cross*, trans. and ed. Kieran Kavanaugh and Otilio Rodriguez (Washington, DC: ICS Publications, 1991), 480.

6. John of the Cross, *St. John of the Cross: Alchemist of the Soul*, ed. and trans. Antonio T. de Nicolas (York Beach, ME: Samuel Weiser, Inc.), 19.

7. The one surviving child of Francisco and Ana became a nun.

Chapter Two

1. Iain Matthew, *The Impact of God: Soundings from St. John of the Cross* (London: Hodder and Stoughton, 1995), 6.

2. See Gerald Brenan, *St. John of the Cross: His Life and Poetry* (Cambridge, UK: University Press, 1973), 6.

3. Saint Albert Avogadro, Patriarch of Jerusalem, who wrote the rule between 1206–1214.

4. The dedication to Mary is not mentioned in the early friars' formula of life, but it seems to have been important to them. The system of feudalism that prevailed in the medieval world saw a lord as the provider and protector for a manor, a landed estate or territorial unit in

which a small community lived and worked. Vassals pledged their dedication to their lord. A lord and his lady together were meant to care for their vassals, who in turn were devoted to them both. Medieval piety saw Jesus as the Lord and Mary, his mother, as the lady who received the devotion of dedicated disciples of her Son.

5. Keith J. Egan, "Carmelite Spirituality," in *The New Dictionary of Catholic Spirituality*, ed. Michael Downey (Collegeville, MN: The Liturgical Press, 1993), 118.

6. Gabriel O'Donnell, "Mendicant Spirituality," in *Spiritual Traditions for the Contemporary Church*, eds. Robin Maas and Gabriel O'Donnell (Nashville: Abingdon, 1990), 83.

7. How much of John's studies were in his own house of studies and how much were in the university is a matter of dispute.

8. *Sayings of Light and Love* 158, in *The Collected Works of St. John of the Cross*, trans. and ed. Kieran Kavanaugh and Otilio Rodriguez (Washington, DC: ICS Publications, 1991), 97.

9. *The Dark Night* 1.10.6. in *The Collected Works of St. John of the Cross*, 382.

10. John later famously taught that three signs indicate one is called to contemplation: "an inability to practice discursive meditation; a disinclination to fix the imagination on other things; the desire to remain alone in loving awareness of God." For this summation of the three signs, see *The Collected Works of St. John of the Cross*, glossary, 768.

11. See Brenan, *St. John of the Cross: His Life and Poetry*, 8.

12. See R. A. Herrera, *Silent Music: The Life, Work, and Thought of St. John of the Cross* (Grand Rapids, MI: Eerdmans, 2004), 39.

13. Matthew, *The Impact of God*, 7.

14. Movement from one religious order to another when one is near the point of ordination was then more common and easily done than in our times of generally more detailed discernment of vocation.

15. See Richard P. Hardy, *John of the Cross: Man and Mystic* (Boston: Pauline Books & Media, 2004), 23.

Chapter Three

1. See Francisco de Osuna, *Third Spiritual Alphabet*, Classics of Western Spirituality Series (New Jersey: Paulist Press, 1981).

2. Charles Healey, *Christian Spirituality: An Introduction to the Heritage* (New York: Alba House, 1998), 258.

3. Teresa of Ávila, *The Book of Her Life*, ch. 8, in *The Collected Works of St. Teresa of Ávila*, vol. 1, trans. Kieran Kavanaugh (Washington, DC: ICS Publications, 1987), 95.

4. Ibid, 94.

5. See Mary Luti, "St. Teresa of Ávila" (Teresa of Jesus, 1515–1582) in *The Modern Catholic Encyclopedia* (Collegeville, MN: The Liturgical Press, 2004), 827–828.

6. Ibid., 827.

7. Matthew, *The Impact of God*, 8.

8. Teresa of Ávila, *The Book of Her Foundations*, ch. 3, no. 17, in *The Collected Works of St. Teresa of Ávila,* vol. 3, trans. Kieran Kavanaugh and Otilio Rodriguez (Washington, DC: ICS Publications, 1985), 112.

9. Teresa of Ávila, Letter 13, to Don Francisco Salcedo, par. 2, in *The Collected Letters of St. Teresa of Ávila*, vol. 1, trans. Kieran Kavanaugh (Washington, DC: ICS Publications, 2001), 60.

10. See Marc Foley, OCD, *St. Teresa of Ávila: The Book of Her Foundations, a Study Guide* (Washington, DC: ICS Publications, 2011), 184.

11. John of the Cross, *The Living Flame of Love*, commentary, st. 3, par. 28, in *The Collected Works of St. John of the Cross,* 684.

12. Teresa of Ávila, *Foundations*, ch. 13, no. 4, 162.

13. Ibid., ch. 13, no. 5, 163.

14. See Kavanaugh, *Doctor of Light,* 90–91.

15. See Hardy, *Man and Mystic*, 28.

16. See Doohan, *The Dark Night Is Our Only Light*, 10.

Chapter Four

1. Teresa of Ávila, Letter 13, to Don Francisco Salcedo, par. 2, in *The Collected Letters of St. Teresa of Ávila*, vol. 1, 60.

2. Tyler, *St. John of the Cross,* 21.

3. John of the Cross, *Ascent of Mount Carmel,* bk. 2, ch. 7, no. 8, in *The Collected Works of St. John of the Cross,* 172.

4. See Brenan, *St. John of the Cross*, 15.

5. *St. John of the Cross: Alchemist of the Soul*, 26.

6. Ruiz, *God Speaks in the Night*, 106.

7. Teresa of Ávila, *Foundations*, op. cit., ch. 14, no. 7, 166.

8. Ibid., no. 12, 168.

9. See Brenan, *St. John of the Cross*, 15.

10. Quoted in *God Speaks in the Night*, 109.

11. From Friar Eliseo de los Martires, quoted in Crisogono de Jesús, *The Life of St. John of the Cross,* trans. Kathleen Pond (London and New York: Longmans and Harper and Brothers, 1958), 306.

12. Quoted in *God Speaks in the Night,* 89.

13. Teresa of Ávila, *Foundations,* ch. 23, n. 9, 220.

14. Brenan, *St. John of the Cross*, 18.

15. John of the Cross, *The Living Flame of Love*, commentary, st. 3, par. 26, 683.

16. Doohan, *The Dark Night Is Our Only Light*, 12.

17. Brenan, *St. John of the Cross,* 18–19.

18. Quoted in *God Speaks in the Night*, 127.

19. See Teresa of Ávila, *Spiritual Testimonies*, no. 31, in *The Collected Works of St. Teresa of Ávila* (1987 ed.), vol. 1, 402.

20. The relocation may have been undertaken to relieve the Reform-minded John of the pressure from less convinced friars at his monastery, or it could have been simply to station the confessors closer to the nuns they served.

21. John of the Cross, *The Living Flame of Love, The Collected Works of St. John of the Cross*, 692–693.

22. John of the Cross, Letter 8, to the Discalced Carmelite Nuns of Beas, in *The Collected Works of St. John of the Cross,* 742.

23. Teresa of Ávila, *The Book of Her Life*, in *The Collected Works of St. Teresa of Ávila*, vol. 1, ch. 8, 96.

Chapter Five

1. John of the Cross, Letter 1, to Madre Catalina de Jesus, July 6, 1581, in *The Collected Works of St. John of the Cross,* 736.

2. Teresa of Ávila, Letter 218, to King Philip II, par. 5 and 6, in *The Collected Letters of St. Teresa of Ávila*, vol. 1, 579–580.

3. John of the Cross, *Sayings of Light and Love*, no. 1, in *The Collected Works of St. John of the Cross.*

4. Quoted in Tyler, *St. John of the Cross*, 31, from P. Silverion de Santa Teresa, *Obras*, vol. V (1929). Juan de Santa Maria's account given at beatification process in Ávila in 1616.

5. Ibid., 32.

Chapter Six

1. Teresa of Ávila, Letter 277, to Mother Anne of Jesus, in *The Collected Letters of St. Teresa of Ávila*, vol. 2, trans. Kieran Kavanaugh (Washington, DC: ICS Publications, 2007), 146.

2. See Nicolas, *St. John of the Cross: Alchemist of the Soul*, 19.

3. John of the Cross, *Sayings of Light and Love*, no. 132, in *The Collected Works of St. John of the Cross,* 95.

4. For more details, see Carmelo Lisón-Tolosana, "The *Beatae:* Feminine Responses to Christianity in Sixteenth-Century Castile," in *Vernacular Christianity: Essays in the Social Anthropology of Religion*, ed. Wendy James and Douglas H. Johnson. (New York: Lilian Barber Press, 1988), 51–59.

5. Practiced largely by converts to Christianity, this heretical movement prized mental prayer (something John and Teresa espoused for those able to enter it), but dismissed the value of vocal prayer (a method John and Teresa staunchly upheld). The *Alumbrados* sought to reach ecstasy through prayer less in order to meet God than for the thrill of the experience. They strove after, rather selfishly, private revelations from God. They disdained a prayer that used words as beneath their level of spiritual attainment. John guided his directees away from Illuminist ideas and toward a steady following of the practices of prayer and virtue found in Catholic spiritual tradition.

The Inquisition found the *Alumbrados* problematic and expressed strong caution regarding any kinds of wordless prayer. The Inquisitors sometimes turned their opposition to the *Alumbrados* into something of a witch-hunt. John, like Teresa, walked a fine line between avoiding the Illuminist ways and defending the value of prayer as authentically something deeper than words could fully express.

6. See Teresa of Ávila, *Spiritual Testimonies*, 64, in *The Collected Works of St. Teresa of Ávila*, vol. 1, 434–435.

7. John of the Cross, Letter 1, to Catalina de Jesús, July 6, 1581, *Collected Works of St. John of the Cross,* 736.

8. Ibid.

Chapter Seven

1. Crisogono de Jesús, *The Life of St. John of the Cross*, 309.

2. Quoted in *God Speaks in the Night*, 234.

3. Ibid., 288.

4. Herrera, *Silent Music*, 44–45.

5. Ibid.

Chapter Eight

1. Quoted in Brenan, *St. John of the Cross*, 65.

2. John of the Cross, *Sayings of Light and Love*, no. 47, in *The Collected Works of St. John of the Cross,* 89.

3. John of the Cross, Letter 26, July 6, 1591, in *The Collected Works of St. John of the Cross,* 760.

4. Brenan, *St. John of the Cross*, 66.

5. John of the Cross, *The Ascent of Mount Carmel*, bk. 1, ch. 13, par. 6, in *The Collected Works of St. John of the Cross,* 149.

6. John of the Cross, Letter 28, August 19, 1591, in *The Collected Works of St. John of the Cross.*

7. John of the Cross, Poem, 11, A Gloss (with a spiritual meaning), in *The Collected Works of St. John of the Cross,* 70.

8. Brenan, *St. John of the Cross*, 76.

9. Quoted in *God Speaks in the Night*, 364.

10. John of the Cross, *The Collected Works of St. John of the Cross*, quoted in General Introduction, 28.

Appendix

1. Crisogono de Jesús, *The Life of St. John of the Cross*, 312.

2. John of the Cross, *The Living Flame of Love*, poem and commentary.

3. John of the Cross, *The Ascent of Mount Carmel*, bk. 1, ch. 2, par. 2, in *The Collected Works of St. John of the Cross*, 120.

A mission of the Daughters of St. Paul

As apostles of Jesus Christ, evangelizing today's world:

We are CALLED to holiness
by God's living Word and Eucharist.

We COMMUNICATE the Gospel message
through our lives and through all
available forms of media.

We SERVE the Church
by responding to the hopes and needs
of all people with the Word of God,
in the spirit of St. Paul.

For more information visit our website:
www.pauline.org.

BOOKS & MEDIA

The Daughters of St. Paul operate book and media centers at the following addresses. Visit, call, or write the one nearest you today, or find us at www.paulinestore.org.